DRESDEN
AND THE
HEAVY BOMBERS

DRESDEN

AND THE

HEAVY BOMBERS

An RAF Navigator's Perspective

Frank Musgrove

Pen & Sword
AVIATION

First published in Great Britain in 2005 by
Pen & Sword Aviation
an imprint of
Pen & Sword Books Ltd

ISBN 1 84415 194 8

British Library Cataloguing-in-Publication Data
A CIP catalogue record for this book is
available from the British Library

Typeset in 10/12pt Palatino by
Phoenix Typesetting, Auldgirth, Dumfriesshire

Printed and bound in England by
CPI UK

Pen & Sword Books Ltd incorporates the Imprints of Pen & Sword Aviation,
Pen & Sword Maritime, Pen & Sword Military, Wharncliffe Local History,
Pen & Sword Select, Pen & Sword Military Classics and Leo Cooper.

For a complete list of Pen & Sword titles please contact
PEN & SWORD BOOKS LIMITED
47 Church Street, Barnsley, South Yorkshire, S70 2AS, England
E-mail: enquiries@pen-and-sword.co.uk
Website: www.pen-and-sword.co.uk

Acknowledgement

I am greatly indebted to Dr Peter Liddle, Director of the Second World War Experience Centre, Leeds, to whom I first sent this memoir for deposit in the Centre's archive. Dr Liddle suggested that it might interest a wider readership and advised me on the possibilities of publication. I am very grateful for this help.

Frank Musgrove

District Target Map
No. G. 82
DRESDEN
(GERMANY)
Illustration No.
D.T.M. G. 82/1
Issued November 1943

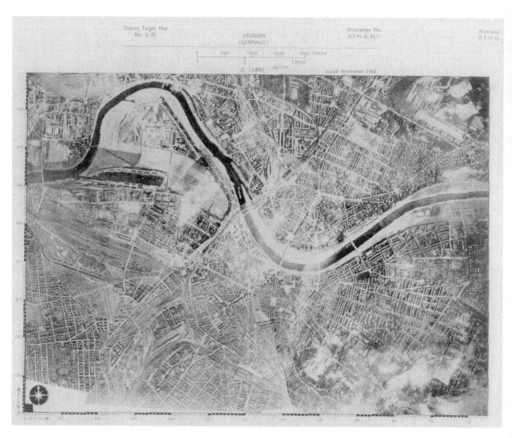

The Dresden Target Map

Contents

CHAPTER ONE

Prologue:
Destructiveness

This is a story that chronicles a young man's entry into war in 1941 and culminates in his flying (as a Lancaster navigator) on the bombing raid to Dresden in February 1945. It offers 'a view from the astrodome' as the bombers' war was seen in close-up at the time, and broader perspectives from sixty years on.

This is not a gung-ho, press-on-regardless, *Boys Own Paper* account of my experience of flying with RAF Bomber Command; but neither is it an exercise in hand-wringing nor breast-beating and avowals of guilt. There is a basic narrative that follows my volunteering for flying duties in the Second World War and eventual membership of a front-line heavy bomber squadron in 1944; it pays particular attention to fear and morale and the myth of leadership. Half a dozen bombing missions are described in some detail, illustrating the variety of experience, problems and dangers involved.

This is a memoir about learning a highly skilled trade (as an air navigator before computers) and applying the basic principles under various conditions and methods of war from the 'area bombing' of Cologne and Dortmund to G-H precision bombing of ball-bearing factories at Solingen, Homberg and Witten. I hope that a reader with little or no technical knowledge will feel that he was actually there and could have done the navigation himself.

A memoir which includes the bombing of factories and cities inevitably raises grave moral issues, which I have also tried to address. I did not feel them very strongly at the time, but they have crept up on me slowly, insidiously, over the past sixty years. Dresden has been invested with huge symbolic significance; and a number of well-publicised books have highlighted its awfulness. Kurt Vonnegut's personal witness account in *Slaughterhouse Five* (1970) and Alexander McKee's *The Devil's Tinderbox* (1982) made a strong impression on me; but David Irving's *The Destruction of Dresden* (1963) seemed grossly overstated. The number of civilian deaths was certainly much smaller than the 135,000 that he estimated. Nevertheless, the probable number, somewhere between 25,000 and 60,000, was certainly grievous (61,000 is the number of British civilians killed by the *Luftwaffe's* bombs in the entire course of the war).

I have wondered why this was a war of unparalleled destructiveness – of people, of property, of values and of institutions. Of course, there were now technical means to be massively destructive, but 'unconditional surrender' as an Allied war aim must carry a large part of the blame. Unconditional surrender leads inexorably to the prolongation of war and to its utter destructiveness: there is no incentive for the side that is clearly losing to sue for peace and the leadership will almost certainly hang. In an age of different and perhaps more chivalric values and priorities, Napoleon in defeat was given a miniature kingdom, a handsome pension and a bodyguard of 400 officers and men. It is true that in 1919 there were cries of 'Hang the Kaiser', but he had taken comfortable retirement in Holland and no-one knew how to extract him or how to hang him if they did.

'Unconditional surrender' was an American import, first given currency by ex-President Theodore Roosevelt in New York's Carnegie Hall in July 1918, and announced (without consultation) by President F.D. Roosevelt to newsmen at the Casablanca Conference in February 1943. Churchill had serious misgivings but to his shame acquiesced. This requirement cut right across European traditions and customs of war.

It is true we required 'regime change' after defeating France in 1814–15 and Germany in 1918, but we did not otherwise impose non-negotiable terms. The defeated nation had recognised representation and an important voice in the final settlement – more so in 1814–15 than in 1918, by which time a distinct hardening of attitude had occurred. The regime change in France in

1814 – the restoration of the Bourbons – was carried out with due sensitivity and engineered by Talleyrand, an aristocratic renegade priest who had actually been one of Napoleon's ministers. (Wellington had recommended this change after sounding out opinion when he reached Toulouse and Bordeaux after his triumph in Spain.) France retained her historic frontiers (as they existed in 1792) and indeed most of her colonial possessions. For twenty-five years France had been a threat to the peace and order of Europe. After revolution at home and the encouragement of subversion abroad came the Terror and then the 'Corsican Ogre' who overran Europe and reached the gates of Moscow. By present-day-standards France was treated with astonishing understanding and, indeed, generosity. There was, however, a very careful and elaborate rebalancing of power within Europe designed principally to deter France from future aggression. These arrangements worked remarkably well for the next forty years.

In 1918 regime change in Germany was demanded more prescriptively and peremptorily: it had to be something that President Woodrow Wilson could recognise as 'democracy' as understood by Americans. When the German high command seemed reluctant to abandon rule by 'monarchical autocrats', Wilson threatened that he would not proceed to a negotiated peace settlement but would accept only (unconditional) surrender.

In fact, movement towards a negotiated peace had been active among the European powers at least since early 1917. Count Albert von Mensdorff-Pouilly, Austro-Hungarian ambassador to London before the war, was in Geneva in December with instructions from his Foreign Minister to discuss possible peace terms with General Jan Smuts, a member of the British War Cabinet. Mensdorff-Pouilly could see no reason why the war should continue: it was precipitating the demise of Europe and the passing of economic and financial power to America. He could not see the possibility of Austria's breaking with Germany, but his exact words were reported by Smuts to the War Cabinet: 'If another year of this destruction has to pass, the position of Europe and civilisation, already so pitiable, would be beyond repair.'

There was certainly widespread unease about the intrusion of American values and power into European affairs; as late as October 1918 Lloyd George was hesitant about ending the war 'too soon', but knew that to continue into 1919 would mean that an American peace would be imposed on an exhausted continent. Even by ending the war in November, America seemed to be claiming a preponderant role in the post-war settlement and this was deeply resented by small nations that had made a disproportionate sacrifice. America had lost about 50,000 men killed; Australia, a tiny nation in comparison, had lost 60,000 killed. (France and Britain combined lost 2,100,000 men killed; Germany lost 1,950,000 men.) Australia's Prime Minister, William Hughes, was deeply resentful: 'If we are not very careful, we shall find ourselves dragged quite unnecessarily behind President Wilson's chariot.'

The degree of manoeuvre in negotiating the peace was indeed more circumscribed than Germany assumed when it agreed to an Armistice on 11 November 1918. The German Army withdrew from France and Belgium in remarkably good shape and did so in the manner of a besieged garrison that had acquitted itself with honour and was now accorded a just and generous peace – allowed to march out with full military honours, with drums beating, flags flying and still bearing arms. This is precisely the way in which the German Army came home from the Western Front, mostly on foot, to reach Berlin by 11 December 1918. Berliners lined the Unter den Linden to cheer the troops who marched in column behind regimental colours with regimental bands. 'I salute you who return undefeated from the field of battle,' declared Chancellor Ebert who was waiting for them in Brandenburger Tor. This was not an army or a government that expected to have little or no say in its eventual fate; and there is no doubt that without such a positive expectation the slaughter and destruction would have continued as a still very capable German Army fought on.

The Germans had their own counter-proposals for a post-war settlement, which they presented to the peace conference at Versailles. They expected them to carry weight and it was on this assumption that they had agreed to lay down their arms. When, in May 1919, their counter-proposals received short shrift, they considered themselves betrayed and seriously thought of restarting the war.

Like the First World War, the Second World War should and could have ended after four years, in September 1943. Two further years of awesome slaughter and destruction need not have occurred. The Battle of El Alamein had been won a year before – useful, but not really of major significance – but the Battle of Stalingrad, which was finally won by the Russians in January 1943, was certainly of huge importance; and so was the Battle of Kursk in July. At Stalingrad, German losses were on a gigantic, indeed, catastrophic scale and the aura of German invincibility vanished. A few months later, as historian Richard Overy has claimed, the struggle for Kursk finally tore the heart out of the German Army. Kursk was the single most important victory of the entire war. Moreover, in May 1943 the German U-boat offensive in the Atlantic had suffered a comparable defeat (forty-one U-boats were sunk out of the ninety or so usually deployed); and in July and August RAF Bomber Command virtually obliterated Hamburg. These three great Allied victories in 1943 – in the Battle of the Atlantic, the Battle of Hamburg and the Battle of Kursk – were body blows to Germany. They could have been the end of the war.

Germany was in fact defeated – not, it is true, to the point of unconditional surrender, but almost certainly, with suitable diplomatic soundings, to the point of seriously and realistically discussing the terms of peace. Post-war retrospective surveys of German morale show that by January 1944, 77 per cent of the sample regarded the war as lost. Why did Germany fight on? Principally because our leaders were exclusively focused on an outcome further down the line – the wholly unconditional surrender that must surely follow a successful 'second front' now well advanced in the planning. In September 1943 the Allies could not see what was before their eyes. This time round, with nothing short of unconditional surrender on the agenda, we really had to grind Germany into the ground.

Even Sir Arthur Harris in his headquarters at High Wycombe did not grasp the full significance of the Battle of Hamburg. Churchill congratulated him on the recent successes of Bomber Command, and Harris still imagined that he could achieve

Germany's unconditional surrender by bombing alone. Hamburg by itself could not accomplish this: it would need 'a Hamburg' inflicted on Berlin. This, he believed, would be the decisive blow. The slaughter must continue.

Of course it is difficult to know when a bomber's battle against a distant enemy has been 'won'. In a land battle the enemy surrenders or retreats: it abandons the fight. A bombed city five hundred miles away in enemy territory can scarcely 'surrender'. Its surviving citizens may put pressure on the government to sue for peace; and this is something that was in fact happening in industrial north Germany before the firestorms of Hamburg had died down. However, by the end of November, when the Allied leaders met in Teheran, the moment had passed for a possible negotiated peace. Stalin, now very confident, was also all in favour of Germany's unconditional surrender and would be pleased, if necessary – and perhaps even preferably – to do it all by himself.

The slaughter and destruction continued on a mounting scale as the Allies suffered serious, repeated setbacks and faltered. Bomber Command's 'Battle of Berlin' was duly inaugurated by Harris and continued throughout the winter until March 1944. This was no Hamburg. It did comparatively little damage, gave rise to grievous RAF losses and, in fact, constituted a major defeat. In January 1944 the Anzio landings, which should have led to the early capture of Rome, turned into one of the most difficult and costly campaigns of the war. The D-Day landings in June were not without heavy losses (comparable to the Somme); in September we suffered the spectacular catastrophe of Arnhem; the Ardennes breakthrough in December brought panic to the Allied armies and all but reversed the achievement of Normandy. The slaughter mounted. In February there were raids on Dresden and Pforzheim, while V1 rockets brought terror to a defenceless London. The Red Army meanwhile continued its horrendous and barbaric drive into the heart of Europe.

An earlier, negotiated peace settlement would have imposed stringent terms and, like the Treaty of Vienna in 1815, would have provided for an effective balance of power within Europe. It might have provided for a significant measure of overall

European integration as Churchill had envisaged in 1940 when he offered actual union with France. It would have maintained the essential integrity of western Europe. There would indeed have been instant 'regime change' in Germany on the clearly established precedent of 1815 and 1918. The price of unconditional surrender, when it eventually came, was the death of a civilisation.

The twenty 'unnecessary' months of war after September 1943 saw the loss of 3650 bombers on missions over Europe and 712 bombers crashed in England. (The months January to April 1945 saw no significant reduction in Bomber Command fatalities: 600 bombers were lost over Europe and 232 crashed in England.) The bomber losses in these twenty months meant more than 25,000 deaths from a Command that never at any particular time numbered more than around 8000 men. These 25,000 deaths need not and should not have occurred.

If in 1918 the Allies had publicly proclaimed that they would accept only Germany's unconditional surrender, there would have been no Armistice on 11 November. The war would have continued until at least 1920 and America would have ruled the world.

CHAPTER TWO

I Volunteer

In the glorious summer of 1941 my schooldays at the Henry Mellish Grammar School in Nottingham were coming to an end. I had taken examinations for a scholarship that would eventually take me to Oxford. The *Luftwaffe* had bombed Nottingham, setting the ancient lace market ablaze and gutting the historic heart of the old town. My return from Oxford (via Birmingham) had been full of high drama. Birmingham came under heavy and prolonged air attack as my train approached Snow Hill station. We stopped and remained just outside throughout the night. We were rocked by bomb explosions and the city appeared to be engulfed in flames. Miraculously we were able to proceed on our way as a new day dawned, eventually reaching Nottingham ten hours late. I arrived home weary from days of examination stress capped by a sleepless night in a railway carriage under heavy aerial attack.

Throughout the summer of 1941 former school friends a year or two older than myself, with whom I had once played rugger and cricket, called in at their old school when they were on leave, wearing their RAF uniforms with pilot's wings. They were uncharacteristically quiet, thoughtful and subdued. The Battle of Britain over Kent and the Thames estuary had been fought and won and Fighter Command was engaged in very costly 'fighter sweeps' over Occupied France; Bomber Command was settling into the long haul of night attacks with Hampden, Whitley and Wellington bombers over Germany. 'I just wish I'd got two engines, and not just the one,' said one of my friends rather wistfully. He was now a Hurricane pilot and felt highly vulnerable and exposed at low level over enemy territory in a single-engined plane. He was lost in a fighter sweep over Normandy a couple of weeks later.

Another friend had become an observer (navigator) on Wellingtons. 'We're lost most of the time,' he said. 'It's a nightmare. Last Friday night I went with the Squadron Leader. He was furious when we seemed to have got nowhere at all at my estimated time of arrival over Bremen. Not even any flak or searchlights. We were bucketing about in the dark, and I was desperate to get a fix or a bearing. The Squadron Leader left the controls with his "Second Dickie", came back and pushed me away from the navigator's table and charts and said he would sort it. But he didn't. We never got to Bremen. I don't know how long we can go on like this.' He was shot down a month or so later and spent the rest of the war as a prisoner-of-war.

A sergeant pilot flying Hampdens from Lincolnshire came in one day: he had been one of the school's outstanding rugger players a few years before. He was delighted to have got to an operational bomber squadron so soon. He talked about a raid on the Kiel Canal which he said had been very successful. His morale, unlike the Wellington navigator's, seemed to be very high. A week later, on the Thursday night, he flew to Lübeck; on the Sunday morning he took up his Hampden bomber on an air test, lost control, crashed on the outskirts of Lincoln and was killed. He had recently married a girl from the Sixth Form of Nottingham Girls' High School. She was pregnant. He was nineteen.

About this time two young bomber pilots, regular officers, came by appointment to talk to the Fifth and Sixth Forms about the work and needs of a rapidly expanding RAF. They gave a laconic, laid-back account of recent missions they had flown to Hamburg and Bremerhaven. They indulged in no heroics. It was not a job for gung-ho, daredevil pilots, they said: there were long, tedious hours of cold and boredom and then sudden action and danger. They said they would be pleased to interview anyone who might have thought of becoming a navigator or pilot. I had absolutely no doubt that this was what I wanted to do, if I possibly could, although I had never been in an aeroplane in my life.

I accepted their invitation. They were interested in my being a member of the First Fifteen and a School Prefect, but even more in my grasp (as an Arts specialist) of logarithms. After half an hour they said they would recommend me for training as a pilot or navigator and signed a certificate of fitness to that effect. It was thus that in 1941 I was accepted for aircrew training in the RAF. However, it was not until 1944 that, as a fully qualified navigator, I joined a squadron of heavy bombers in East Anglia.

In the summer of 1941 when the young bomber pilots came to my school, Britain stood entirely alone against the might of the all-conquering Third Reich. It was now a year since the British Army had retreated from Europe via Dunkirk: the possibility of getting an army back into Europe was nil. Russia was attacked by Germany on 22 June and Churchill in a momentous broadcast pledged to the Soviets our unreserved support. But Russia at that point seemed to be a serious liability rather than any help and was widely expected to suffer early defeat. It we were to continue the war against Germany, it would have to be from the air.

It was not until late 1942, after completing my first stages of training in England, that I arrived as a senior cadet at the advanced school of air navigation in South Africa. I was one of a course of thirty men, mostly in their early twenties, who had been accountants, university students, teachers, bank clerks and company directors. Throughout the following frenetically busy year I progressed from bewilderment and near despair in the air to reasonable competence in my trade. My closest friend on the course was a bank clerk from Surrey. He was very anxious. 'Making up the accounts and balancing the books at the end of the week at the bank put you under immense pressure,' he said, 'but at least if you got it wrong you weren't actually killed. But in this job you are'. In fact, he did get it wrong and one night appears to have given his pilot a course which took them head-on into the Drakensberg mountains.

Navigating a relatively slow, twin-engined Anson aircraft in South Africa was not the ideal preparation for bombing Germany. The technology was primitive: the Ansons were not even fitted with an intercom. Communications between crew members were written on message pads and passed around by hand. (The crew were a pilot, trainee navigator and wireless operator.) There was no oxygen for higher altitudes and of course no heating. There was no radar. Air navigation was essentially age-old sea navigation, crudely adapted to problems and conditions at 10,000 feet travelling at around 170 mph instead of at sea level travelling at 12 mph. It all depended on laboriously plotting a course on a Mercator's map which, after allowing for wind speed and direction would enable you to follow a particular track. (The 'course' was the direction you set on the compass and flew through the air, but the 'track' was the route you actually made good over the ground.) The key to navigation is knowing the wind speed and direction; but there is no instrument like the anemograph that can give you this in flight. (The aircraft is making its own wind which falsifies any measure that might be made.) Wind speed and direction can only be inferred from other information, preferably from knowing where you actually are and where you should be. The distance and angle between them is the measurable wind effect.

In the air, flying often bumpily at nearly 200 miles an hour, we did what mariners had done for two or three centuries in the relative spaciousness and leisure of their craft: we took compass bearings of headlands, transposed position lines on our charts to bring them to the same time, 'doubled the angle on the bow' and obtained a 'fix'. At night we took (often highly inaccurate) star shots with sextants and made elaborate calculations from the relevant entries (for time and date) in air almanacs. By the time we had taken the shot, made our calculations and obtained a position line (we were somewhere along its length) we were probably thirty miles from where we began. However, we actually needed shots of two different stars and two position lines: our actual position was at the point where the two would intersect. By now we had moved on another thirty miles and we still hadn't calculated the wind.

These were hectic, almost frantic, days and nights of flying on a wide variety of carefully contrived exercises: obtaining fixes from bearings and from pin-point observations of the ground; calculating ground speed and track-made-good (between two fixes) and so inferring wind speed and direction; observing sea lanes as we flew over the Indian Ocean and calculating 'two-drift winds'; and most intellectually challenging of all, the astrofixes. On these night exercises we were often completely lost, but at least the African night sky was a friendly sky, and I could usually identify the larger towns below like King Williams Town, Grahamstown and East London. Our phlegmatic South African pilots flew the courses calculated by their trainee navigators into a frightening void.

What I recall clearly is not the danger but the anxiety, unrelenting pressure and harassment of navigating in these peaceful sub-tropical skies. Even more vividly I remember the sheer physical discomfort of clambering around the Anson aircraft in sub-zero temperatures to take the various measurements and readings. All the work could not be done at my navigator's desk. Wearing full flying kit (because of the cold) it was necessary to move to various observation points to take note of the sea lanes below, to use the sextant and to take bearings of landmarks. To take a compass bearing, for example, I struggled over the main spar to the rear of the Anson, extended a bracket through a window in the fuselage, mounted a compass on the bracket, and then, as the aircraft pitched and rolled, peered out into an icy airstream to some remote (and hopefully correctly identified) headland. I then clambered back to my desk and drew a position line. However, I then had to climb back to the rear window to take a second reading for another position line, which, in conjunction with the first (appropriately transposed for the time that had elapsed), could provide me with a fix. By now, at five or six thousand feet, I was extremely cold and utterly exhausted.

Our navigation instructors in South Africa were mostly 'resting' from the war in the Western Desert where they had flown Wellingtons along the north African coast to bomb Benghazi and Tobruk: extremely hazardous, but a navigator's dream in its sheer simplicity. It was no induction at all into the sophisticated strategies and skills required to fly from eastern England through the featureless waste of night-time, blacked-out Europe to bomb Essen or Hanover. Nevertheless, by the time we graduated from the South African air school we had a very sound grasp of the basic, timeless principles of navigation, whether on the sea or in the air, although our acquaintance with the latest scientific technology was minimal. We were also learning quickly that the air navigator's war, wherever it is fought, is never predictable and routine, but calls for constant improvisation, inspired judgments (informed guesswork), with few blessed moments of certainty and none of repose.

The officer in charge of my course was a very down-to-earth Lancastrian in his mid-thirties who had been a rubber planter in Malaya and had flown as a navigator on Wellingtons in the Western Desert. He had no wish ever to return to England. 'I suppose you all wanted to be glamour-boy fighter pilots,' he would say. 'But you're not. You're navigators. You'd better get used to the idea.' It is true that we had all volunteered originally for 'flying duties' but we knew that whether we became pilots or navigators depended on our aptitude and the exigencies of war. Our commanding officer was determined to drive home the message that air navigation was a vital but essentially un-glamorous calling. In truth, I had never for one moment envisaged myself as a fighter pilot and was delighted to have been chosen for navigator training. However, I should have been bitterly disappointed to be a bomb-aimer, which I always considered a non-job and held in complete contempt. And still do.

The pilots who flew the Ansons at the school of air navigation were white South Africans with no combat experience. None of them had been into battle; all of them were 'non-operational'. The navigation instructors were Englishmen, New Zealanders and Australians who had been in the thick of the fighting in the Western Desert. Tension between them and the South African pilots, who were often their superiors in rank, could be bitter and public. For one of the great divides in a wartime air force – apart from the basic structural separation of ground staff and aircrew – is between those (fully qualified) pilots and navigators who have flown in battle, and those who have not. A trivial dispute (over lecture room allocation) between a South African pilot who had never been north of the Limpopo and a New Zealand navigator who had repeatedly faced the formidable defences of Tobruk, erupted into a public affray. 'I'm taking no orders from you, you non-operational bastard,' declared the New Zealander, who was of inferior rank. He was promptly placed under arrest and disappeared to await court martial.

Throughout 1943 we closely followed the war news from home. We were eager for information about the great battles that raged at Stalingrad and Kursk, which clearly had profound implications for the future course of the war. We noted with some concern the huge losses that Bomber Command appeared to suffer night after night. In the early months of 1943 there were usually about twenty aircraft lost on a night-time bombing mission to Germany: in April twenty-three Lancasters and Halifaxes were lost over Stuttgart and twenty-one over Stettin. But later in the year numbers rose steeply. What was later to be known as the Battle of Berlin had begun: sixty-two heavy bombers were lost over Berlin on 23 August and forty-seven on 31 August. Losses continued at the same level until the end of the year. Forty bombers were lost on 2 December. In our NAAFI breaks we began to talk about the 'chop rate' over Germany and developed a line of ironic gallows humour. Some cadets were clearly beginning to have second thoughts and to wonder why they had ever volunteered; and a few were seriously thinking of a way out.

We were getting to know white South Africa well and to appreciate its manifest attractions. White families (mostly of English and Scottish descent) organised a hospitality scheme in East London and cadets in twos and threes were invited to their homes for Sunday tea or even for the weekend. The scheme had existed for more than a year and most families had come to know quite well a stream of aircrew cadets and followed their subsequent careers back in England. These were usually all too brief. 'You remember Peter, the blond young man who had been to Harrow,' said our hostess to her husband over tea. 'He was a first-class tennis player, charming man. He flew on half a dozen big raids when he got back to England, but we heard last week that he'd been killed over Mannheim.' They were full of the young men they had known, some of whom had become engaged to, or even married, their daughters. Although we were known as 'the blue plague', an ever-present danger to both wives and daughters, their recollections were full of pride. But the recollections all ended the same way: killed within six months or so over Nuremberg, Frankfurt or Hamburg. It became depressing. After five or six weekends I dropped out of the hospitality scheme.

The delights of South Africa were becoming ever more enticing. There was no black-out, no rationing, no bombs; there were golden beaches without barbed wire. There was swimming and tennis, abundant fruit, endless fried bacon and eggs, and gorgeous suntanned girls in swimming suits. Bomber Command was losing some of its appeal. The senior cadet on my course, who had a First in Mathematics from Balliol, married the daughter of a newspaper proprietor in Durban and contrived to stay on as an instructor.

I had little sense of social tension and virtually no exposure to black South Africa. The Afrikaaners (Boers) in general were not in favour of our war against Germany, but were remarkably hospitable. When we once made a forced landing in atrocious weather in a field near Graaf-Reinet, we arranged with the local police for an armed guard to be put on our aircraft overnight. This was not for protection against the Bantu but against the Boers. However, the Boer farmers in and around the town treated us with great friendliness, fine Cape wines and brandy and generally lavish hospitality. We were there for four days until the weather cleared up. I still have very fond memories of Graaf-Reinet.

To be grounded for medical reasons or even incompetence and relegated to the ground staff as a mechanic, meteorological assistant or drill instructor was quite inviting. We observed with some envy the cushioned, luxurious lifestyle of the fit young English ground staff who serviced the aircraft or were PTIs and the like, had married local girls and 'lived out'. One cadet claimed to have developed eye problems that made it impossible for him to use a sextant or take compass bearings. Another discovered that he had, after all, a poor head for heights and was impossibly dizzy, disoriented, uncoordinated and unable to concentrate above 2000 feet. It was easiest to fail the exams. We were examined in cartography, meteorology, 'dead-reckoning' navigation, astronavigation, armaments, signals, and the principles of flight, and assessed for practical competence in the air. Failing all or part of the course was not unduly difficult, and repeated failure meant being grounded. We knew that the likely reward for examination success was incineration in an exploding Lancaster at 20,000 feet over Mannheim or Stettin. Few examinations can have had stronger disincentives built in. In the circumstances a failure or wastage rate of less than 5 per cent was impressive.

At the end of the course in South Africa we were fully qualified RAF navigators, but some three or four months further training in the latest methods of air navigation were needed before we could join bomber squadrons and fly over Europe. We were made senior NCOs: only one cadet out of thirty was offered a commission. By late 1943 there was some caution in granting commissions to young aircrew as yet unblooded by war. If they refused to fly when they got to the battle front in Europe – and a not insignificant number did – they were more difficult to deal with if they held the King's commission. NCOs could be dealt with in more summary fashion, reduced to the ranks and assigned to menial duties. I received the King's commission after I had joined a heavy bomber squadron and bombed Germany.

CHAPTER THREE

The Real Thing

Early in 1944 I was posted to an OTU (Operational Training Unit) near Kettering for some three months' training on Wellington bombers before finally joining a front-line squadron. When I arrived, a Wellington lay awkwardly in a ploughed field across from the guard room: it was nose-down into the ground, tilted over onto a crushed starboard wing. 'What's happened here?' I asked the guard-room corporal. 'It crashed last night returning from a cross-country navigation exercise,' he replied. 'All the crew were sitting unmarked in their seats, dead, when we got there – except for the rear-gunner, who just walked away from it.' Now, I thought, we are getting near to the 'Real Thing'.

The Real Thing was more than sudden death on a training exercise – I had seen this before in South Africa (in fact accidents on training flights accounted in the course of the war for some 10,000 deaths). The Real Thing was a bomber with an intercom, a piped oxygen supply to a face mask, radar (especially 'Gee'), radio silence (so as not to give your position away) and an API (Air Position Indicator). It was blacked-out Britain, night flying with no visual guidance or clues, your own permanent crew with whom you lived on terms of close intimacy, friendship and friction, and with whom you would probably die. This was the preparation for bombing missions and aerial combat over Hitler's Third Reich.

Gee and the API were instruments of huge significance for the navigator. The former was a radar device for obtaining a fix (where you actually were), and the latter was a computerised system that converted course and airspeed into the position you 'should' be in: that is to say, where you would be if there had been no wind. The difference between the former (your 'ground position') and the latter (your 'air position') was the wind effect.

The API was in many ways the more important of the two: without laboriously, and often inaccurately, plotting the courses and distances you had flown on your Mercator's chart, you could now read off from the API the coordinates of the position you 'should' be in. It was also mercifully free from any ground interference and other sources of error. If you do the plot manually but the pilot does not fly the courses you give him accurately and at a constant speed, your calculated air position will be grievously wrong. And so will everything else: inferred wind speed and direction, ETAs (Estimated Times of Arrival) at turning points and target, and calculated courses to fly.

The trouble with Gee – which gave you your ground position – was that the radar signals were easily jammed. It was a navigational system based on a grid of signals transmitted from England, which were received as two parallel, horizontal lines of 'blips' on a cathode-ray tube (a TV style screen). The navigator used his Gee controls to align the upper and lower blips (thereby, in effect, placing his aircraft at the intersection of two position lines). He could then read off the coordinates of the fix. It could all be done quickly and very accurately, giving the aircraft's position to within a mile or so; but enemy interference (on the same frequencies) made the Gee sets virtually inoperable before crossing the Rhine.

The API was subject to no such interference, but you had to know the wind speed and direction and 'lay-off' the wind effect from the position that the API gave. Wind speed and direction were still the unknowns, which somehow had to be found. There were no soft options or (literally) quick fixes when you got to the Real Thing.

Over blacked-out Britain and Europe, the navigator probably never saw the ground between take-off and landing; he probably never even looked – there was no point. Conventional map reading was impossible: at more that 20,000 feet, some four miles above the ground, even on a clear moonlit night, there would be few landmarks down below that could be easily identified. A distinctive stretch of coastline or a major river was the only exception. Map-reading skills were useless and in fact I never carried a detailed topographical map, like an Ordnance Survey map. My basic tool was an 'empty', very parsimonious Mercator's chart, an outline map without distracting detail, on which the route to the target, track-made-good, fixes and air positions could be clearly marked.

The Mercator's map actually distorts the Earth's surface and distances across it, because the lines of longitude have been straightened out and the ground correspondingly 'stretched'. The lines of longitude have been made parallel and do not converge towards the North Pole. A straight-line course from west to east therefore cuts all lines of longitude at the same angle, which greatly simplifies the navigator's task. In reality, a straight line – the shortest distance between two points – would cut lines of longitude at different angles and involve frequent course alterations. The Mercator's projection introduces distortion and error for navigational convenience. However, in the relatively short distances we flew over Europe, the errors were not on a significant scale.

The navigator worked in a curtained cubicle with his Gee set, API, plotting table, rulers, dividers, protractors, portable calculator, air almanacs, and Mercator's chart. His astrodome with a sextant – for possible use in dire navigational emergencies – was a Perspex 'blister' in the fuselage above his head. Standing in the astrodome gave a magnificent view of a target under attack.

In South Africa it had usually been possible to identify major towns at night, ablaze with light: a string from Port Alfred on the coast inland to Graaf-Reinet, Somerset East and Beaufort West. There were no such possibilities and felicities now. In the sub-tropical night skies of the southern hemisphere in 1943 air navigation could, at times, be an unalloyed delight.

At an OTU you formed the nucleus of a permanent crew – pilot, navigator and bomb-aimer. These were the 'professionals'. Two gunners (rear and mid-upper), a signaller (an airborne wireless operator) and flight engineer were the 'tradesmen' (although they might be of superior rank). They had come into the RAF by a different route, having volunteered for these particular trades, and they joined the nucleus later. The basic crew members were not detailed by some higher authority: they were self-selecting, coming together informally, even casually; but once the choice was made it was permanent. It was one of the most important decisions these men would ever make in their lives.

Some twenty or so newly qualified pilots, twenty navigators and twenty bomb-aimers had arrived together at the OTU and over the next few days they met together in the mess, the lecture rooms and in coffee breaks and began the informal process of sorting themselves out. I talked to a rather intense and studious English pilot (he always seemed to carry a huge flying manual around) who had already come to an agreement with a bomb-aimer. We got on well and provisionally agreed to crew up. But I hesitated. I was approached the next morning during a coffee break between lectures by two blond, broadly smiling, handsome Australians. Johnny, a pilot, was in his mid-twenties. He was a young journalist from Sydney. Jack, a bomb-aimer, a good ten years older, was a civil servant from Melbourne. Would I join them (they had obviously talked me over and decided on a joint approach)? My instincts said: Yes. I agreed on the spot. This casual-seeming, almost random decision was one of momentous importance.

Johnny, the pilot, was an outgoing extrovert, a great party man. I am quieter, more inward, more deliberative, less spontaneous. He talked too much and was inclined to exaggerate; I talked too little and tended to minimise. We complemented each other well; but under great stress we were probably impatient and not always understanding of the other's quite different response. Johnny had great skill and pleasure in action, his responses were quick and well coordinated. However, under great stress he was shrill, impatient, verging on hysteria, often physically exhausted. My more introverted temper and quieter (but no less terrified) responses provided a balance which on the whole made for an effective crew.

That evening, after we had formed our embryo crew, we went to the Three Swans in Market Harborough. We drank great quantities of ale (and only with great difficulty rode our bicycles back to camp). We talked a little about our lives before joining the Air Force – but sketchily, economically. We never knew a great deal about one another; we withheld our more private, personal lives. Our relationships were cordial, good-humoured, respectful of our different skills, but never very close. The loss of a crew member through death or injury (or refusal to fly) would be temporarily disturbing; but it would not devastate our lives. Unconsciously, defensively we held our past lives and deeper thoughts and feelings in guarded reserve. Even Johnny the extrovert revealed remarkably little about himself. Our conversation was mostly 'shop'.

A few weeks later all the crews flew on a practice night-bombing-exercise over the Wash and a nearby bombing range. Bombing, whether in training or over a German target, was always a tense and clumsy affair. With the bomb-doors open the aircraft was difficult to handle, vulnerable, its aerodynamic properties impaired. It seemed to stagger in the sky, and when the bombs were released the aircraft rose steeply and unmanageably higher into the sky. The studious pilot, with whom I had so nearly crewed up, apparently lost control and crashed. He and his crew were killed. I felt only huge relief that I had followed my instincts and joined my (slightly alien, rather loud) Australian friends.

At the OTU we became proficient in front-line tactics and technology: a far cry from the rudimentary, basic, navigational skills we had acquired in South Africa. The great Berlin raids were now taking place and we were aware of the formidable challenge that lay ahead. In fact, Bomber Command was losing the battle: its losses were simply unsustainable. More than 600 heavy bombers were lost in nineteen major raids – that meant nearly 5,000 young men killed.

In the early hours of 31 March the bombers were streaming back from Nuremberg: ninety-five (we learned later) were missing. At about 6 o'clock a badly damaged Lancaster, with its port engine shot away, made an emergency landing at our OTU. We were at breakfast when, after debriefing, the crew came into the mess, still in flying kit (we carried no change of clothes or even shaving kit). They looked dazed, dishevelled and exhausted; they were very quiet and subdued. No one knew yet of the scale of the losses sustained that night, but the Lancaster crew spoke briefly and bitterly of a massacre over Nuremberg and on the way home. ('I plotted the position of Lancs that exploded, one after another, as we headed desperately for home,' the navigator said. 'I plotted more than twenty, and thought we'd be next.') Our training was almost over now. We should be joining a front-line squadron soon.

The long period of training had, in fact, in the context of the times, been a thoroughly demoralising experience. Looking back, I am astonished that so few aircrew volunteers (and we were all volunteers) backed off. Among those I knew who did 'back off' were two of my friends who later became highly distinguished Cambridge University dons.

CHAPTER FOUR

Dortmund and Leipzig

The nights of 6 October and 6 December 1944 remain for ever sharply etched in my memory: on the first the target for my Lancaster squadron was Dortmund; on the second, Leipzig. But these German cities were simply coordinates on a map of Europe, the first relatively near, involving around six hours of flying, the second depressingly distant, involving some eight or nine hours of flying. Both sets of coordinates were at the centre of areas shaded deep red on our maps to indicate heavy defences. For me 'Dortmund' and 'Leipzig' had no further substance or concrete reality. But 6 October was the night we were 'coned'; 6 December the night we were struck by lightening. These are the short, sharp, dramatic realities that remain with me and give these nights shape and a distinctive identity.

On 6 October I went down to breakfast and looked as a matter of course at the mess notice board. Among various announcements there was a dance in Thetford town hall on Saturday night and a Battle Order for a bombing mission to Germany. Twelve of the squadron's eighteen available crews were on the list and mine was one of them. There was, of course, no mention of the target (a carefully kept secret until the crews had their final briefing some seven or eight hours later). The navigators' briefing was timetabled for 3 o'clock, the main briefing for the assembled crews at 4 o'clock. I concluded that take-off would be around six.

At breakfast no one mentioned the Battle Order; the talk was all about the dance in Thetford. We discussed how we could organise some transport to get there. The American crews from the Flying Fortresses based near Long Melford would be there in force, with smooth talk and plenty of money; but we would put on a show.

Throughout the day twelve Lancasters were prepared for their mission that night. News filtered back from the ground crews at the dispersal points around the airfield of the weight of fuel, bomb loads and bomb types. If the fuel was abnormally heavy and the bomb load relatively light (mostly incendiaries), we were likely to be flying to the far eastern region of Germany. As the day wore on we concluded with some relief that we were going to a middle-range target: we would be carrying 'block-busters' and a few incendiaries. Our surmise was correct: it would, in fact, be Dortmund.

Briefing, pre-flight planning (calculating courses in advance on the basis of forecast winds), take-off and the outward flight were routine and unremarkable. The meteorological officer had given the navigators forecast winds for different heights and areas between East Anglia and the Ruhr, and the navigators had calculated the courses their pilots must fly to make good the different 'legs' of the route. These would have to be checked and corrected by obtaining Gee fixes as far as Gee cover extended – hopefully to the Dutch coast and perhaps for some considerable distance beyond. I settled to my task of obtaining fixes, calculating winds, revising courses and ETAs as we climbed steadily to operational height at 20,000 feet over the North Sea.

It was a singularly black night. After taking off and climbing to 2000 feet as we circled the airfield I saw nothing whatsoever for the next two-and-a-half hours: only my maps, navigational instruments, rulers and dividers on the table of my dimly lit compartment. I hadn't felt the 'bump' as we entered the slip-stream of a neighbouring aircraft, which would indicate that we were dangerously close but at least flying the same course as somebody else. I began to think we were totally lost. As we approached my ETA at Dortmund the world outside was simply a black void. My last Gee fix was more than half an hour ago. By now the sky should be livid with flak and an inferno should be visible four miles below.

And then I saw a dull red glow on broken clouds some way ahead. I felt a huge surge of relief: thank God, we were heading

Frank Musgrove in flying kit during early 1944.

An Avro Lancaster Mk I being stripped down and serviced in preparation for her next operation. Twelve groundcrew are visible; to keep a bomber flying demanded the skills of a large number of personnel in addition to the aircrew. *(Philip Jarrett)*

A Lancaster Mark III of No. 149 Squadron. *(Philip Jarrett)*

Bombing-up. Under the great bomb-doors is a four-thousand pound bomb with other heavy bombs and incendiaries on the train. *(Philip Jarrett)*

Seen here in the bitterly cold winter of February 1944, work goes on to keep the Lancasters ready for night-raids into Germany. On one bomber station the RAF Regiment cleared the runways continually for two days. *(Philip Jarrett)*

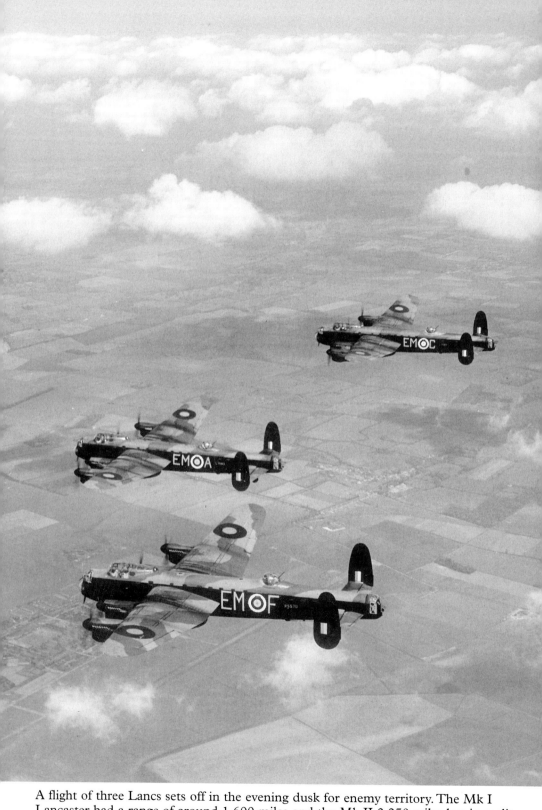

A flight of three Lancs sets off in the evening dusk for enemy territory. The Mk I Lancaster had a range of around 1,600 miles and the Mk II 2,250 miles but in reality this would vary with the bomb-load and the weather conditions. *(Philip Jarrett)*

The Lancaster defended itself with machine guns mounted in the nose and tail, an upper gun-turret and sometimes in a position below the fuselage. At night, it was tail-end Charlie who was relied upon to spot enemy nightfighters whose favourite ploy was to sneek up on the aircraft from slightly below and astern. *(Philip Jarrett)*

When flying above dense cloud the navigator relied upon radio navigational aids or dead reckoning. It was a hazardous affair. *(Philip Jarrett)*

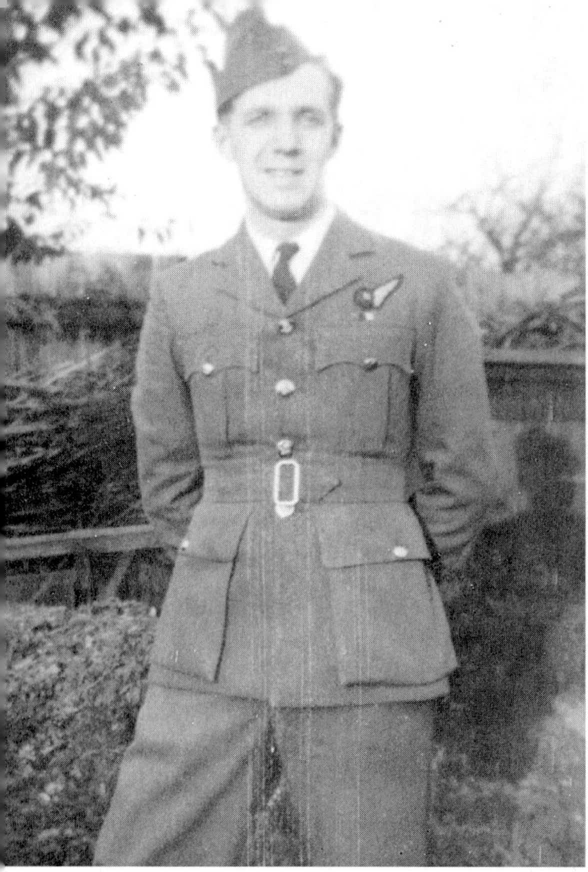

Two photos of Frank

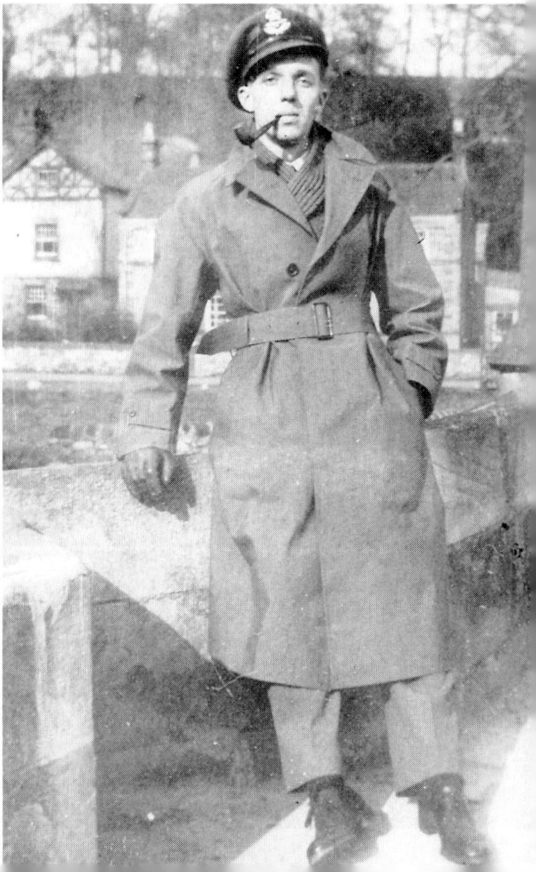

A view from the tail-turret. This type of loose formation was adopted on the outward and return flights – close enough for mutual protection against *Luftwaffe* fighters but sufficiently spaced to allow the pilot to fly the aircraft without the undue stress and concentration required when closed up tight.

(Philip Jarrett)

With a wing span of 102 feet, the Lancaster could carry a cargo of bombs weighing 22,000 pounds – a payload that was far heavier than for the target. Suddenly, we were in brilliantly illuminated space high above the Ruhr, with myriads of searchlights criss-crossing the sky. I took my portable parachute down from its rack and clipped it onto my chest. I worked at my charts, calculating an up-to-date wind for the bomb-aimer to set on his bomb-sight and a course to get us most directly out of the target area once the bombs had been dropped. Light flickered through the window of my curtained compartment, brilliantly but fleetingly illuminating my charts. We were flying bumpily, the pilot sweating and asking impatiently, 'How much longer?' The bomb-aimer replied soothingly, 'Nearly there, steady skipper, steady. Starboard a bit, starboard . . . yes, steady.' Then I realised that my cabin was flooded with light. The searchlights were not flicking over – they held steady. We had been 'coned'.

To be coned over a heavily defended target is a singularly desperate predicament. Your aircraft has been picked out by the ground defences for concentrated attention until it is finally destroyed. All – or the vast majority – of Dortmund's search-lights had swung on to us now, holding us brilliantly illuminated, twisting and turning, in a cone of light. All – or most – of the flak batteries were directed at us too.

Other crew members also had a very lively appreciation of our plight, especially the gunners. 'We're coned, skipper, dive,' the rear-gunner's Lancashire tones, urgent but calm. The bombing run was abruptly, indeed violently, abandoned as we dived at something over 300 mph ('indicated' airspeed) and lost four or five thousand feet. My ears were acutely painful and I thought my eardrums would rupture as we made this precipi-tous descent. The searchlights still held us securely while anti-aircraft guns mustered their concentrated fire, and the sky around cascaded with exploding shells.

Then suddenly we were not in the cone. My compartment was no longer brilliantly lit and I could scarcely see my charts. We levelled out, turned onto the target markers and continued our bombing run. 'Bombs gone, skipper.' Suddenly, ten tons or so lighter, we lifted unnervingly into a sky full of unseen Lancaster bombers. 'Course 262 degrees, Johnny,' I said, and the pilot began to swing the aircraft round onto a westerly, homeward course. 'Christ, that's suicide,' came Johnny's startled voice. I looked out from my astrodome: ahead of us, across our west-ward course, there was an apparently solid wall of searchlights and flak. 'OK, Johnny,' I said, 'Just turn north and fly out of it where you can. I'll give you a new course when things settle down.' The aircraft swung north and ten minutes or so later we entered blissfully black space and continued onwards towards the Baltic Sea.

We were, in fact, making ourselves highly vulnerable. By detaching ourselves from the main bomber stream, we could be more easily picked off by fighters. But we did not feel more vulnerable; we felt safely enveloped by the dark night, blessedly distant from Dortmund's searchlights and flak.

The Ruhr defences were roughly triangular, with a broad base across the Dortmund – Essen region, tapering south to an apex at Düsseldorf and Cologne. At Dortmund we were on this area's outward, northern edge. A north-westerly course would take us quickly well clear of the Ruhr. An uneventful half an hour or so after leaving Dortmund I saw a coastline below, which I could identify as the south-eastern corner of the Zuider Zee. This was a rare visual fix, from which I could now plot a new track that we must traverse back to East Anglia. My API was still working and I could calculate a new wind and the course that the pilot must fly.

I suddenly felt extraordinarily tired as we flew across the North Sea. My lower back ached, and I lay down for twenty minutes or so on my long navigator's bench. There was a little idle chatter on the intercom, light banter as the crew relaxed. We reached our base without further incident. It was still scarcely midnight when we came into land.

We touched down gently, but then lurched over onto our port side, slithering to rest on the wing, which burst into flames. All our internal lighting failed. I groped my way to an emergency exit over the starboard wing, pulled it open and climbed out. Once on the wing I jumped. It was much higher from the runway than I'd thought. I bruised my lower spine, and although the damage was not serious, I never sat easily again for more than an hour or so – on railway journeys or in examination rooms – for more than twenty years. I got to my feet and ran as the Lancaster exploded. All the crew got out.

When the wreckage was examined the next day, it seemed that flak had damaged our undercarriage and one wheel had failed to descend when we came into land.

Our flight engineer – the youngest crew member, aged only nineteen – refused to fly again. He quickly disappeared from the station. I never knew where. I never enquired.

The remaining six of us got to the dance in Thetford on Saturday night.

A night two months later remains etched on my memory after sixty years for a quite different sequence of events. It was a night in early December when we were briefed to go to Leipzig, but met catastrophe before we had lifted more than a few hundred feet from the ground.

There were three targets for Bomber Command that night: Osnabrück, Giessen, and the oil refineries at Leuna, near Leipzig. My squadron was detailed to attack the oil refineries near Leipzig.

Targets in the far eastern region of Germany were always viewed with some apprehension. There was the longer exposure to fighters and flak, the sheer physical strain of flying eight or nine hours instead of five or six to targets in central and western Germany; and above all the greater problems of navigation. The reputation of the eastern targets was awesome. Berlin, Nuremberg and Stettin had taken a heavy and well publicised toll of Bomber Command's crews. One of the heaviest losses of the war had occurred on a raid on Leipzig on 19 February 1944, when seventy-eight heavy bombers were lost – over 9 per cent of those despatched.

When we assembled for our main briefing at 4 o'clock we already knew that we would be flying to a distant target. Information about fuel and bombs had filtered back to the mess throughout the day. When the Wing Commander unveiled the map no one was unduly surprised to see that the track we were to follow led via a number of dog-legs to Leipzig. However, one crew was clearly deeply disconcerted. The men sat bunched closely together, talking quietly, as the briefing proceeded. They then rose together. 'We're bloody well not going,' one of them announced. The crew had flown twenty missions and the last two had seen the men suffer severe damage, a crash landing and their bomb-aimer killed. They walked out of the Leipzig briefing and refused to fly again.

Tension among the eighty young men in the briefing room was palpable, but the briefing continued and navigators made their pre-flight calculations. The meteorological forecast was not promising: we were to expect a good deal of turbulence, dangerous cumulo nimbus cloud and electric storms. It was dusk as we climbed aboard our Lancaster bomber and the sky was dark blue and threatening.

Our heavily laden Lancaster ran down the runway at half past five and rose sluggishly into the sky. We would circle the airfield until we reached 2000 feet and then set course for Clacton. I was arranging my navigator's table, securing my Mercator's chart, with the tracks and turning points clearly marked, checking the setting on my API (the longitude and latitude of the airfield), and about to fine-tune my Gee set when suddenly it exploded. Fragments of the cathode-ray tube were all over my plotting table, and the aircraft violently shuddered and lurched. I felt sickeningly weightless. The aircraft was clearly out of control and we were barely 1000 feet high.

Johnny's heavy breathing and grunting could be heard over the intercom as he and the flight engineer struggled to regain control. 'My God, we've been struck by a thunderbolt' – the bomb-aimer said. This was it – we would hit the ground with our full fuel tanks and bomb load any second now. We would probably hit the village church. But our fall was abruptly halted; the aircraft began to pull up and a babble of voices burst over the intercom. 'I'm blind,' said the rear-gunner, 'my guns have been struck by lightning.' The mid-upper-gunner was in a similar plight: blue light had run down his guns and the metal was electrified. Instruments had exploded or became erratic and unreliable. There was no question now of our proceeding to Leipzig. Could we even get down safely at base?

When an aircraft has been seriously damaged and is highly unstable in flight, there is a powerful urge simply to get out of it, especially among the peripheral, more 'detached' members. This applies especially to gunners, in their isolated turrets, who don't really know what is going on. 'Climb up to 5000 feet, Johnny, and let us all bale out,' said the mid-upper-gunner. But we were flying more steadily now and in no immediate danger. 'I'll get a course for the North Sea dumping area,' I said, 'We must get rid of the bombs.'

So we set course for an area of the North Sea designated for emergencies of this kind, where excess fuel and bombs could be jettisoned. But the gyro-compass was now unstable and unreliable. I mounted my astrocompass (which functions independently of the Earth's magnetic field) on its bracket in the astrodome and aligned it with Polaris. It would provide a rough check on the course we were flying. On this stormy December night as we flew north-eastwards over the sea to release our bombs, Bomber Command Lancasters and Halifaxes were heading for Osnabrück, Leipzig and Giessen.

We came in to land an hour and a half after we had taken off, badly shaken. The gunners in particular were in shock. They had been literally stunned when the lightning struck their guns and temporarily blinded. But it was still only about 8 o'clock when we handed in our parachutes and climbed out of our harnesses and flying gear. Time to get down to the village pub. By 9 o'clock we were drinking our first pints. We talked and laughed a little too loudly. Our friends wouldn't have reached Leipzig yet.

Twenty heavy bombers failed to return from their targets in Germany that night.

CHAPTER FIVE

Fog and Fido

E ast Anglia and the Fens in wartime seemed remote and inaccessible. The blistering heat and violent electric storms of high summer gave way as autumn approached to a watery and ghostly landscape of mist and sometimes impenetrable fog. All flying then was cancelled. The black-and-white villages and small towns withdrew into themselves, but their pubs were warm and comforting and lay at the very heart of Bomber Command. They nurtured crew cohesion and were a crucial factor in morale.

We flew three missions in conditions of heavy fog and were unable to return to our base, either being diverted to a fog-free airfield elsewhere in England or to an emergency landings strip with fog-dispersal facilities. Looking back now through the mists of sixty years these missions tend to coalesce in my mind. They lack the clear definition of a daylight raid in cold, clear-blue skies high over northern Germany. It was like flying in soup. One mission I remember only very sketchily, although it was of considerable tactical importance. The German army's ferocious Ardennes breakthrough was made under cover of heavy fog and General Eisenhower asked the RAF for support. Only a G-H attack could provide blind-bombing with the pin-point accuracy that would hit German troop concentrations but miss our own forces nearby. We provided these attacks with stunning effect and Eisenhower congratulated Bomber Command on its 'magnificent performance'. I remember only a dim and murky experience and a message saying we could not land at our fog-bound base.

The mission that I flew to a target near Coblenz in early November 1944 was another rather indeterminate, fog-bound raid, but enlivened by a little more incident. The meteorological officer warned us at the briefing that there could be some mist or fog when we returned, but he thought it would not be a serious problem. In the event we came back to densely befogged airfields and nearly a hundred heavy bombers with dangerously low fuel tanks desperately made emergency landings. With only minutes to spare we finally landed on FIDO (Fog Investigation Dispersal Operation) at Woodbridge.

We had started to get very edgy for some weeks before this: raids had been repeatedly cancelled, the mid-upper gunner was developing a nervous skin disorder, and we were becoming bored. An RAF station deep in the countryside of East Anglia in still autumn days is singularly lacking in excitement. We played chess and cards. In the evenings we were probably spending far too much time in the pub.

The Oak was comfortable and relaxed, a welcoming place for all ranks to meet on terms of equality and informality. Most Lancaster crews were a mix of senior NCOs and junior commissioned officers: the NCOs ate and lived in the sergeants' mess, the rest in the officers' mess. This demarcation was potentially threatening to the cohesion and wellbeing of the crew. In the Golden Fleece's bar differences in rank were of no account and crew solidarity was sustained.

Senior officers (of field rank) were seldom there – they certainly wouldn't 'make a night of it'. However, ground staff personnel were there, and so were locals – the butcher and his wife, the blacksmith and his daughter. Aircrew tended to stand apart – not from any sense of superiority, but because they were less deeply rooted in the community and their ties to it were comparatively light.

Ground staff might be stationed there for years – they were armourers, fitters, cooks and mechanics. Aircrew were transient; in any event they would not remain there when they finished their tour, and might well be killed or missing long before that. They were an element of instability and flux in a relatively settled social order. A sergeant fitter would sit with his girlfriend and her mother in the place of honour by the fire in the bar; pilots, navigators and gunners were more likely to cluster together, a little apart, by the door in the cold. Bonding and cohesiveness between ground staff and aircrew is essentially a myth of post-war films.

I remember no drunkenness. Spirits and wines were not available; in an evening we drank two, perhaps even three, pints of watery beer. The atmosphere was convivial but seemly. (Far more inclined to excess and dangerous to our health was the remarkable number of cigarettes that we smoked.) Crews on RAF stations near cities like Cambridge, Lincoln and York had access to more sophisticated amenities, were less drawn to village inns and more inclined to paint the town red. They were often roughly handled by RAF military police. These 'city' crews also seemed to have a particularly high 'chop rate'. In the depths of rural Lincolnshire and Yorkshire the tempo was quieter. Looking back now on the village pubs and their aircrew clientele, I recall only an astonishing sobriety.

The crew was becoming restless and ill-humoured. For some even flying on bombing missions over Germany simply extended and replicated boredom on the ground. Flying at night at high altitudes is in fact a boring business: once you have climbed to operational height, levelled out and settled on a course at a constant speed, there is no sense of speed. The gunners would sit for hours staring out into space, but whereas in the mess they would be bored and warm, now they were bored in temperatures well below zero. Nobody spoke to them on the intercom: why should they? The signaller listened in, but for hours received no messages, or none of great consequence. We would be shaking about in a cold metal box four miles high. It was a silent world. Even when shells exploded around us, we saw the fireworks but heard little or nothing. (I often wondered whether I could have endured the sheer noise of battle as an infantryman.) The four Rolls-Royce Merlin engines indeed filled the aircraft with sound, but apart from take-offs and landings and occasional emergency manoeuvres en route, it was a constant and unnoticed, remaining at the same volume and pitch. Sudden changes in pitch can be alarming: have we been hit? Most of the time, however, the Merlin engines were reassuring and comforting.

The bomb-aimer was likely to be particularly bored, lying for hours on his stomach in his forward compartment with nothing to do. The pilot, the flight engineer and the navigator had most to occupy them in normal flight. The flight engineer had a complex system of fuel tanks to manage and monitor; as the navigator I was particularly lucky because I was always under pressure, endlessly busy, never bored. By contrast, the bomb-aimer had a serious job to do only in the half hour or so as we approached the target, when in effect he assumed supreme command. Once we were over enemy territory, it is true, he pushed out bundles of 'window' – strips of aluminium foil that would confuse German radar and suggest that there were far more bombers than was actually the case. But this was repetitive, menial work – a labouring job performed by an RAF commissioned officer for hours towards the target and then for hours on the return to base.

In theory the bomb-aimer was also an air-gunner. The Lancaster had three gun turrets: a rear turret with a rear-gunner; a mid-upper turret also with a 'resident' gunner; and a front turret in the nose of the aircraft, which was invariably vacant. (Curiously, there was no under-belly turret which would cover attacks from below – the most common.) The vacant front turret would, it was assumed, be manned in emergencies by the bomb-aimer; but the time when such emergencies were most likely to arise was in the run-in to the target when the bomb-aimer was very seriously otherwise engaged.

Our take-off was quite late at night (11 o'clock) and our route was somewhat convoluted. We were to fly a hundred miles across the North Sea as if heading for Bremen before turning south-east and proceeding by a series of dog-legs to the upper Rhine valley. We would be in the air for about six hours, returning in a crisp autumn dawn to a breakfast of ham and eggs.

As we climbed over the North Sea the bomb-aimer decided he would check out the front turret and test his guns. It had never occurred to him or anyone else that he should do so before; but tonight he was adamant. This was simply a nuisance, a distraction for all of us, but test them he did and, to his own satisfaction, fired them off around the North Sea.

Our bomb-aimer's response to frustration and boredom was really quite muted. The tedium of flight could have more dramatic consequences. One dawn while we returned from an attack on Essen, two Lancaster pilots ahead of us began high-spirited manoeuvres until finally the aircraft were leapfrogging over each other. I watched this show with amusement and indeed admiration and then with horror: one of the Lancasters collided with the other as it tried to fly over; the two aircraft became enmeshed and plummeted into the sea. They had survived Essen, but boredom as we flew back – or perhaps it was relief or even elation – had brought them to an untimely and watery grave. My own guess is boredom. There is no tedium much greater than flying, once you are well clear of the target, on auto-pilot.

Over Coblenz one of the Merlin engines suddenly began to scream: a highly discordant and disconcerting invasion of our silent world. The engine was not on fire but had apparently been hit. The flight engineer said that the engine must be switched off and 'feathered' (the propellers adjusted to the wind so that they would not 'windmill'). We pulled away from the target on three engines and headed for home.

However, it was not only an engine that had been damaged: our ASI (Air Speed Indicator) had become highly erratic and was registering impossible speeds. This was likely to prove a more serious problem over the next few hours than an engine out of action.

The speed of an aircraft is measured by the air pressure that builds up on its wings as it flies. The greater the speed the greater the pressure – an apparently simple and straightforward relationship. The air pressure registers in an open-ended tube (pitot head) that projects forward from the wing, and is converted into speed at miles per hour (or knots) on an ASI on the control panel in the cockpit and in the navigator's compart-ment. If the forward-projecting tube becomes blocked or damaged, the ASI will give an inaccurate reading (or in extreme cases no reading at all). We appeared to have at least a minor problem of this kind as we headed back to England.

In any event the IAS (Indicated Air Speed) is not the TAS (True Air Speed) – neither of course is it the ground speed. The difference between your 'indicated' speed and your 'true' speed through the air becomes greater the higher you fly. The air becomes colder and thinner, the pressure on the pitot head is less than it 'ought' to be, and the ASI under-reads. The pilot flies in accordance with the speed shown on the indicator, but the navigator must know the true speed. He will have to correct the indicated speed to allow for reduced air pressure at greater heights. The TAS may well be 30 or 40 mph greater than the IAS. However, without a reliable indicated speed to start with, his correction will be pointless; moreover, the automated API (Air Position Indicator) will give you a false air position because it has been fed inaccurate information. Quite clearly, apart from a defunct port-inner engine, we had problems.

I decided to keep a manual air plot, drawing the courses flown and the air distances travelled on my Mercator's chart. This was certainly not a complete or perhaps adequate solution. The airspeed I used for this purpose would be a best estimate, somewhere near the speed the Lancaster would normally fly. It seemed to be the best improvisation and protection against the vagaries of an aberrant API that I could achieve.

About ten minutes after we had left the target the signaller received one of the rare messages of any significance that he ever got calling for some sort of action: there was heavy fog over East Anglia and we were diverted to Dishforth in north Yorkshire where conditions were good. I calculated that we were now near Leige and drew a new track direct to Dishforth – a distance of around 400 miles, nearly 100 miles further than our base in Norfolk. We now had a serious problem of fuel consumption, too. We should be getting quite low on fuel by the time we reached north Yorkshire.

As we came near to my ETA for Dishforth we were flying at around 5000 feet but could see nothing of the ground. The signaller then received another message of importance: there was now fog at Dishforth and we must land at the emergency airfield at Woodbridge in Suffolk. We now had to fly back for another 100 miles. The flight engineer consulted with the pilot about our fuel supplies: we all heard the exchange on the intercom. He was clearly a very worried man.

Woodbridge was an emergency airfield virtually on the Suffolk coast with greatly extended runways and a FIDO instal-lation for lifting fog. The runway was 3000 yards long and aircraft with damaged hydraulics might be able to get down and safely come to a halt in the greater-than-normal space available. FIDO was a technology developed in 1943 and installed early the following year. It was a system whereby long pipes fed vaporised petroleum to burners, which produced a pure flame of intense heat that lifted the fog. The burner pipes were laid parallel with the runway and about 50 yards from it. They extended along each side of the runway and into the approach area. The heat cut a channel through the fog, and although there was a good deal of turbulence, the pilot had a clear area in which to land.

We came in bumpily with little fuel to spare. The fog was still dense. We left the Lancaster at a repair bay and went to sample the very basic amenities that Woodbridge offered. We were very tired. After some breakfast we relaxed in a rather Spartan mess. It was now twenty-four hours since we had got up to face a day of preparation for a six-hour mission to Coblenz. It was not clear when we could return to base.

Woodbridge received around 4200 aircraft in a state of emergency in the sixteen months or so before the war ended in 1945. Both American and RAF aircraft landed there either because they were badly damaged, had defective controls and needed an extended runway to get down, or because fog prevented their landing anywhere else. Soon after midday the fog began to lift but American Flying Fortresses were suddenly arriving, damaged on early daylight raids. There was utter chaos and carnage. Seven Fortresses came in crippled, on fire, with crew members wounded and dead.

Ambulances and fire-tenders stood by. As one Fortress came in steeply with an engine on fire and its tailplane virtually blown away, three figures jumped out one after the other. Their parachutes did not open in time. They hit the ground and were killed. They had apparently decided that they were going to crash badly and their best chance was to get out while they could. One was the navigator, a colonel who had commanded the raid. Two other Fortresses collided as they lurched across the runway. At Woodbridge you saw a fearful concentration of the day's severest casualties which could (just) remain in the air.

By now we were very tired indeed, but our Lancaster would

take some days to repair. We were to be provided with a jeep to take us back to our base. We had lived through the previous day of mounting tension as we prepared for the forthcoming raid. Was it really only yesterday? We had made careful, highly skilled and demanding preparations according to our different responsibilities and trades. We were going into a major military action, equivalent to a battle in which an infantry soldier might fight. (We fought thirty such battles – considerably more than most front-line soldiers in the entire course of a war.) It was time that we got some sleep.

We waited for our jeep to arrive. We looked dishevelled, disreputable, in need of a shave. We all still wore our flying gear and carried our parachute harness, portable parachute and flying helmet with its oxygen mask, and (in my case) a large, green canvas 'goon bag' with my mathematical instruments, maps and charts. We drove away from the high drama and constant crisis of a FIDO landing strip to be swallowed up once more into the deep peace of East Anglia's misty lanes and village pubs.

CHAPTER SIX

Wind

On the night of 23 December 1944 my squadron was briefed for a bombing mission against a target near Bonn; in the event we never got there (although I believed that we had) but instead bombed the railway yards at Cologne. When my aerial photographs of our bombs' point of impact were later developed, this was abundantly clear. My 'misplaced' bombs were no particular loss to Bomber Command's effort that night: both Bonn and Cologne were designated targets marked by flares dropped by Path Finder Force. However, we had, unwittingly, exposed ourselves to very high risk by joining a small group of bombers that came under ferocious attack. As we made our bombing run into Cologne, a Lancaster pilot, Squadron Leader Palmer, now mortally wounded, was in the process of winning a posthumous Victoria Cross.

The mission against the railway yard at Cologne was a precision attack on an Oboe-marked target carried out by a small force of twenty-seven Lancasters and three Mosquitoes. This was (in percentage terms) one of the most costly missions of the war. The defence was particularly strong and five Lancasters and one Mosquito were brought down, 20 per cent of the force that had been dispatched. Palmer's gallantry was later testified by his rear-gunner, who survived. The aircraft was badly damaged as it approached Cologne and Palmer was grievously wounded, but he kept his crippled and now blazing Lancaster on course and made a perfectly controlled bombing run to the railway yards. He then went down with his aircraft; only the gunner got out. We had joined this high-cost attack on Cologne and failed to reach Bonn because we were some twenty-five miles off course. Over the past two hours I had miscalculated the wind.

There are two basic requirements of navigation: knowing from time to time (at least every hour, and preferably every twenty minutes) exactly where you are; and (equally important) knowing how to get from where you are to somewhere else. For the first you need a fix; for the second you need to know the wind. ('Knowing the wind' means knowing its speed to within 4/5 mph and the direction from which it blows to four or five degrees, as in 57/352°.) Wind-finding by navigators was the key to Bomber Command's failure or success.

In 1944 there were four methods by which the navigator of a heavy bomber might obtain a fix: visual identification of landmarks; using a sextant to obtain the altitude of stars and so calculate an astro-fix; Gee; and H2S. The last two were ingenious applications of radar to the problems of navigation. Gee depended on receiving signals transmitted from England, but they were routinely jammed by the enemy; H2S was airborne radar that scanned the ground and reflected back a rudimentary, outline map onto a cathode-ray screen. It could not be jammed. But it had a serious disadvantage: enemy fighters could 'home' in on it and by using it you were more likely to be killed.

In practice, by 1944, the navigation of heavy bombers over Germany at night depended entirely on H2S and Gee. All heavy bombers were equipped with Gee, but the majority of bombers were not equipped with H2S (all the Lancasters of Path Finder Force were). Even in 1944, in spite of these impressive applications of modern science to the problems of air navigation, a high proportion of a bomber force could still bomb fifty or sixty miles from where they should have done. This was because Gee had a limited (and unpredictable) range and H2S fixes were often simply not good enough. H2S provided only a very fuzzy and imprecise image of the ground below. A town showed up as a dark smudge on the screen, but if you did not have a pretty good idea of where you were anyway, you wouldn't know whether it was Düsseldorf or Cologne, or even Leipzig or Schweinfurt. Not knowing where you were wasn't crucially important; not knowing the wind speed and direction in your particular part of the sky, with some precision, certainly was.

The meteorological service provided forecast winds for all heights up to 20,000 feet and for all parts of the route. These were certainly useful, indeed indispensable, for pre-flight planning, but could be disastrous if taken too much on trust. They had to be revised as you obtained your fixes and abandoned altogether if the winds you were finding were significantly different. You had to have the confidence to trust your own calculations.

The forecast winds were provisional estimates and could be seriously in error. Under the limitations of wartime forecasting, and especially through inadequate data from continental Europe, predictions were not only imprecise but sometimes radically wrong. A frontal system over central Europe through which the bombers would fly might go entirely undetected. When a navigator began finding winds from 190 degrees at 70 mph instead of the predicted winds from 20 degrees at 30 mph he would begin to doubt his own calculations and perhaps fudge a wind somewhere between the two. The result could be calamitous. Instead of flying thirty miles clear of Hanover he would be taking his crew through the middle of its formidable defences. And if he escaped from Hanover, would be unlikely ever to get to his target in Magdeburg.

Finding the wind speed and direction in the dark over Europe in 1944 was a far cry from wind-finding as I had known it in daytime over South Africa in 1943. But the principles were the same. The stakes, however, were rather different. I recall with great pleasure flying down from Pretoria to Bloemfontein in an Anson at 5000 feet. In the clear light of the High Veld, long straight strings of light-grey smoke were attached to remote Arfikaaner farmsteads below. The strings lay at right angles across my track, and I knew it was blowing from the east. I had been calculating winds of 30 mph from the north and realised that my courses and ETAs must be wrong. As we crossed the Vaal river near Klerksdorp I was able to pin-point my position and obtain an accurate fix; my air position was shown on the air plot (of courses flown) that I had carefully and laboriously maintained. The distance and direction between the fix and the air position enabled me to calculate an accurate wind and revise my courses and times. However, in 1944 no such leisurely, languid procedure was possible in the night skies of Germany.

The great Leipzig raid of December 1943 illustrates well the tragic consequences of inaccurately calculated winds. More than 500 Halifaxes and Lancasters made a highly successful attack on aircraft production plants in the city. The bomber stream flew out on a direct route across Holland and Germany as though to attack Berlin, but then turned abruptly southwards to Leipzig. The Germans had alerted their night fighters to assemble over Berlin; Leipzig was provided with no adequate fighter defence. Only four bombers were lost.

On the return flight twenty heavy bombers were lost. The designated route home was over relatively undefended territory between Cologne and Frankfurt, and the forecast northerly wind was fairly light. However, the wind was not in fact 30 mph as the meteorological service had predicted, but 60 mph and a significant number of navigators had failed to calculate its true strength and were twenty miles off their intended route. They flew over the heavy flak defences of Frankfurt, with calamitous results.

The losses incurred on the ill-fated Nuremberg raid of 30 March 1944, when 95 heavy bombers were lost, arose in part from similar circumstances. Out of 782 bombers dispatched that night only 512 bombed Nuremberg; a significant number – probably around 120 – bombed a secondary target for the night, the heavily defended ball-bearing factories 55 miles to the north-west at Schweinfurt. The remaining 150 bombers attacked neither Nuremburg nor Schweinfurt, but unidentified targets elsewhere. It was a gigantic shambles. The upshot was a widely scattered bomber force for the homeward flight: instead of a reasonably compact stream five to ten miles wide, it was more like 100. The bombers had passed through a major wind change and navigators differed in their calculations by as much as 50 degrees in wind direction and 50 mph in speed.

The bombers that had attacked Schweinfurt believed they had bombed Nuremberg and navigated accordingly. By now the originally compact bomber stream (which, for a force of that size was about 90 miles in length anyway) extended over a frontage of more than 100 miles. It was in fact a huge 100 mile square box of unwieldy and disorientated Halifax and Lancaster bombers, moving across the night skies of central Europe. Within this vast box of widely dispersed bombers the German night-fighters roamed freely, picking off the bombers at will. More RAF fliers were killed in that single night than throughout the entire six months of the Battle of Britain. Miscalculated winds had taken an awesome toll.

The night of 24 March 1944 was the night of the Big Wind; and it was the night when 810 heavy bombers set off from England to bomb Berlin. The forecast wind over the North Sea was 21 mph from 340 degrees, and over Germany at 20,000 feet, 44 mph from 358 degrees. But over Germany navigators were calculating winds of more than 100 mph and for the most part simply didn't believe the figures. How could the expert forecasters be wrong by more than 60 mph? They fudged their winds when they calculated their courses and ETAs. Sixteen bombers were lost over Berlin. As the bombers turned for home they became scattered over a 150 mile front. Fifty-six bombers were lost on the way to the coast. This loss was not on quite the same scale as would happen on the Nuremburg raid a week later; but in the space of a week, miscalculated winds had made a large contribution to the death of more than a thousand young men.

My own miscalculation of the wind on 23 December 1944 was rather more modest in scale and far less serious in its consequences. However, it was much more culpable, because it was not a deep-penetration raid like Leipzig, Nuremburg or Berlin, but a raid to a medium-range target near Bonn. My error was 25 miles. However, my initial error was magnified on the homeward flight. I had reset my air-plot (my API) with the longitude and latitude of Bonn, and so began my return flight with a 25-mile error. I was still seriously underestimating the strength of the wind and was much further south than I thought. When I should have been crossing the English coast near Yarmouth I was somewhere around Brighton. I was now getting accurate Gee fixes again, however, and somewhat tardily found my way home to Norfolk, by now becoming somewhat puzzled as to where we had actually been.

The navigator's work – indeed, his life – had a high degree of unreality: the wind was not something that blew in his face; the track-made-good was not a path he felt under his feet; the turning point was not a fork in the road, the end of a hedgerow, or a clump of trees. The wind he wrestled with in his dimly lit, isolated compartment, was a vector in a triangle of velocities, which it was his business constantly to address and repeatedly solve. One side of the triangle was course and airspeed, another was track and ground speed, and the third was wind speed and direction. It was the relationships among these variables with which he had to deal. The triangle was a tidy abstraction from a confused, tempestuous and utterly chaotic reality. It was this triangle of abstractions which, in the tumult of battle above the inferno of a German city, defined the boundaries and limits of his world.

CHAPTER SEVEN

God and G-H

I flew on thirty bombing missions. This was the 'contract' for aircrew with Main-Force heavy bomber squadrons. The concept of a limited 'tour' was of immense importance: it afforded reasonable, if not high, hopes of survival. It was the very bedrock of Bomber Command morale. By comparison, 'leadership', of any kind, from any quarter, was an irrelevance.

Twelve of the thirty missions I flew were against 'conventional' industrial targets, including Essen, Dortmund, Cologne and Nuremburg: all were carried out at night and a 'Master Bomber' of Path Finder Force used his sophisticated navigational aids (H2S and Oboe) to locate the target and mark it accurately with flares. The Lancasters and Halifaxes of 'Main Force' then bombed the TIs (Target Indicators). (Of course, the TIs drifted in the wind, and new ones had to be put down. The Master Bomber remained over the target and redirected the bombing onto new clusters. It is remarkable when I think of it now that none of us knew who this courageous man was, or even his deputy who took over when he announced that he'd been hit and was going down. The total anonymity of this unseen 'leading from the front' was taken for granted, unremarked. All we ever saw or knew of this Master Bomber was his Lancaster 15,000 feet below, silhouetted as it moved across the target's flames.)

The other missions that I flew had quite a different character. One was a low-level, army-support daylight attack on a concentration of German troops; the other seventeen were precision attacks on oil refineries and ball-bearing plants using a new navigational aid known as G-H.

There was no Master Bomber on the G-H raids. Each Lancaster

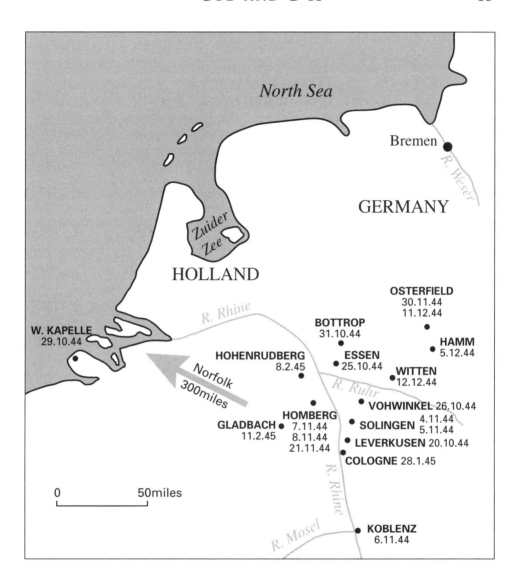

G-H PRECISION (BLIND) BOMBING
(Steelworks, synthetic oil plants and railway yards)

navigator used radar signals to locate the target; no visual identification was made and the bombing was 'blind'. It was nevertheless remarkably accurate. The signals that were transmitted from England could be received by only a relatively small number of bombers, around 100, so these were not the mass raids with up to 800 bombers of the recent past. G-H missions were flown both by day and by night. They were medium-range: the system was effective about as far as the Ruhr but not much beyond.

The G-H missions were hazardous. The targets were usually oil refineries or (less often) ball-bearing factories, which were vitally important to the German war effort and therefore strongly defended. Among the oil refineries that I attacked in the course of 1944 were plants at Leverkusen and Homberg and the Meerbeck works at Bottrop; among the ball-bearing factories were Solingen and the Ruhrstahl works at Witten.

There was an overall decline in the number of bomber losses from the spring of 1944 to the summer of 1945; but at times the casualty rate could be spectacular. A night attack on Gelsenkirchen on 12 June resulted in seventeen Lancasters lost out of 286 (6.1 per cent); nine days later an attack by 130 Lancasters on the oil plant at Wesselring saw the loss of thirty-seven bombers – a dramatic 28 per cent of those dispatched. On 21 July a raid on Homberg saw comparable losses: twenty out of 147 Lancasters were lost (13.6 per cent). Twenty-nine heavy bombers were lost at Stuttgart on 28 July and twenty-three at Stettin on 29 August. Both the Gelsenkirchen and Homberg losses were incurred attacking oil plants by conventional target identification and marking by Master Bombers. But now the G-H force based in East Anglia was virtually taking over the oil offensive with generally highly satisfactory results.

The attack on German troop concentrations near Calais in which I took part on 24 September should have been easy. Somewhat more than a hundred heavy bombers took off from their bases in eastern England around 3 o'clock on a mellow autumn afternoon to converge on Calais at half past four. They would fly out and bomb at 2000 feet. The navigation was easy; the distance made no heavy demands on pilots and crews; the weather over England was good. Each bomber carried ten tons of bombs. That was one of the problems. Another problem was the terrifying concentration of more than a hundred bombers, all at exactly the same low level, converging on a relatively small patch of French soil still in enemy hands.

Here was a still very active pocket of heavily armed German troops that had been left marooned as the Allied armies advanced. It was a troublesome enclave behind our lines and had stubbornly refused to surrender. Bomber Command in all its might was called in to obliterate it.

As we flew low over the corn fields of eastern England the late-September afternoon was golden; but there was low cloud ahead across the Channel and as we approached Calais our target was only patchily visible. The plan was that the Master Bomber would pinpoint the target with TIs to assist visual identification; but in the event this was impossible and there was sheer chaos in the sky over Calais and Cap Gris Nez. Lancasters were desperately trying to avoid collision. Many were turning away without dropping their bombs, and the rest bombed erratically. We did not fly in formation (we never did); there were no 'leaders'; it was the usual scrum. As our bombs fell we felt a succession of deep thuds, powerful blasts reaching up to our aircraft and sucking it down; but we kept our height and flew on through a barrage of light flak. Lancasters were exploding around us. One Halifax and seven Lancasters were lost: a significant percentage from a small force of bombers flying an easy mission.

G-H was a new target-location radar system that came into use with a dozen or so selected squadrons in the summer of 1944. It was used in attacks at 20,000 feet. Signals were transmitted from England, which 'marked' the target and could be picked up by a hundred or so bombers when they were in the target area. (They were provided, as it were, with a pre-calculated fix onto which they could home.) The Gee equipment had to be reset by the navigator to receive new sets of signals (two horizontal parallel lines of blips): he had to fit a different cathode-ray tube. In order to operate Gee as distinct from G-H, the navigator used his tuning controls to move upper and lower blips into line. By contrast, in the case of G-H he moved the aircraft – he calculated a sequence of courses to fly (he was actually flying a curve) and the blips came into alignment as the target approached. The moment the blips came together the bombs were released.

All this meant a frantic half hour at a time of maximum danger. When the bombs had gone and the pilot was pulling steeply away from the target, he dismantled the Gee-set again and replaced the original cathode-ray tube. The usual weaving and diving would be taking its normal violent course amidst the searchlights and flak.

Out of the seventeen G-H missions that I flew, two stand out particularly vividly and I believe that I remember them in every technical and human detail. One mission was to Homberg on 21 November, the other to Witten some three weeks later, on 12 December. Both were daylight raids carried out at 20,000 feet in clear winter skies.

On 21 November we were on the Battle Order that had been posted up in the mess, but Johnny our pilot was quite ill and unfit to fly. Our Commanding Officer (CO), the Wing Commander, said he would step into his place. I had mixed feelings: the Wing Commander was a regular officer and certainly an accomplished pilot; but he was a stickler for form and did everything 'by the book'. At this stage we did not know what the target was (although the Wing Commander as CO would have had this information). It turned out to be the oil refineries at Homberg. The Wing Commander had certainly not picked an easy target – Homberg had an unenviable reputation. I had been there twice before and the flak had been formidable. I had no wish to go there again. But we took off in mid-morning into a bitter-cold blue winter sky.

We rendezvoused with a hundred other Lancasters over Yarmouth and climbed to 20,000 feet over the North Sea. I obtained Gee fixes and calculated winds every twenty minutes. Accurate wind-finding was particularly important for the success of G-H raids (we had no Master Bomber marking the target for us) and as we ran into the target area all the navigators communicated their last wind to a navigator-coordinator who calculated the average out and transmitted the result back to all the bomb-aimers. The same, up-to-date average wind was then set on every bomb-sight; and the bombing concentration achieved was devastating and the accuracy unusually high.

I was busy adapting my Gee-set and calculating courses and winds. I had clipped my portable parachute to my chest, extraordinarily uncomfortable when working over a cramped plotting table, but ready in case we were hit and I could get out. I gave the Wing Commander a course into the target and he held the aircraft rock-steady, when a voice I identified as the mid-upper gunner's said over the intercom: 'A Lanc overhead, skipper. He's got his bomb-doors open. He's right above us.' 'Oh, he'll see us and move across,' said the Wing Commander. I stood up and looked out through my astrodome. To my horror I saw bombs beginning to fall – vast, ungainly canisters falling in slow motion. They couldn't possibly miss our aircraft. But they did. One fell on one side of the fuselage: it seemed only a foot or so clear; another fell on the other side, likewise a foot or so clear; but a third seemed to be falling in slow motion directly towards the rear-gunner's turret. It missed the turret and the gunner and struck the tailplane; it was, of course, fused but it did not explode. However, it took a large section of the tailplane away. 'I thought it was going to land in my lap,' said the rear-gunner. (He was a man in his mid-thirties, a Co-Op manager from Burnley. He was always laconic, cheerful, utterly fatalistic, and unflappable under attack.) We had all had – so far – an astonishing escape. But the aircraft was destabilised; and with ten tons of bombs still on board we went into a sickening dive through a great barrage of flak, down towards the fire and flames of Homberg's oil refineries below.

The Wing Commander at last pulled the Lancaster out of its dive at around 12,000 feet; and he continued straight and level into the target. Our bombs were released precisely on time.

The question now was: Can we get home? The Wing Commander thought that we could. The aircraft was very difficult to control and we were highly vulnerable to any fighter aircraft that might come our way; but the Wing Commander flew the emergency course I had calculated straight back to base. No dog-legs now. I expected to fall out of the sky at any moment. But we got back safely, were debriefed, told our story, and went over to the mess. Johnny came into the mess to welcome us back. He had heard all the details. Was he, perhaps, just a little

disappointed that we had survived? His tour was not now interrupted, perhaps indefinitely, until he could find a place with a
new crew.

The Wing Commander had flown skillfully and calmly and
kept the aircraft flying when a less experienced and capable pilot
would have baled the crew out. But our own pilot, Johnny,
would never have got us into this predicament in the first place.
Flying steady, straight and level, whatever is happening around
you, is the text-book recipe for an effective bombing run. It's also
a recipe for disaster. Johnny would have been sweating and
swearing, weaving around, reacting quickly to danger. He
would have veered rapidly and steeply away from the bomber
as it moved overhead, although his bombing run would have
been less than perfect. Our pilot on 21 November showed an
astonishing unawareness of what was happening around him.
He was decorated for his bravery in action over Homberg: for
his handling of a crisis which was of his own making.

There was, moreover, no sense in which the Wing
Commander was leading the raid or even his squadron of fourteen bombers. He was leading neither by instruction nor
example. He was certainly not leading from the front: along with
another hundred aircraft he was anonymously embedded somewhere in the scrum. Nobody, in any event, would be aware of
which aircraft he was flying, and other squadrons would not
even know that he was on the raid. (Most of his squadron probably didn't know either – and certainly didn't care.) He gave no
order or signal to other aircraft regarding any manoeuvre or
action to take. (As usual we maintained absolute radio silence
between aircraft, apart from communicating technical information about winds.) His steady run into the target and his
response to the damage his aircraft sustained, would be an
example and inspiration to no one. If anyone even noticed it,
they would have no idea who was flying the plane. We were not,
of course, flying in formation as the Americans did, with senior
officers in the lead. We were simply part of an unwieldy,
seething mass of aeroplanes flying in highly dangerous, un-
regulated proximity. Wing commanders and sergeant Pilots
were as one.

'Ops' or operations were quite often cancelled, even when the preparation for take-off was well advanced. In fact, on no fewer than four occasions we were briefed for heavily defended oil targets but at the very last moment were 'stood down'. There was some sense of anticlimax, but the relief was always immense. Unexpectedly severe weather conditions reported along the route, or a suspected intelligence leak that would put defences on high (and appropriately located) alert, might be the reason for cancellation. The telephone in the briefing room would ring, the duty officer would take the call and then announce that the raid was off. Telephone calls might have nothing whatsoever to do with cancellations, but there was always a slight air of expectancy when the telephone rang.

Once, a briefing for an oil refinery target raid was well advanced. All the crews were assembled in the briefing room for the latest information on weather conditions and any special problems along the route. The telephone rang. The duty officer took the call, put down the receiver and announced. 'Sorry, chaps. It's off'. There was a resounding spontaneous and un-inhibited cheer. Crews left the briefing room, shed flying gear for smarter apparel, and headed for the surrounding villages and the Golden Fleece and the White Swan.

On 12 December we went to Witten. This turned out to be a much more horrific experience than the Homberg raid three weeks earlier. Again we flew in a bitterly cold blue sky four miles above the north German plain. But as we approached Witten we saw in the distance, high over the target, a small cluster of black gnats. As we got nearer we saw that they were not gnats or even birds (we never really thought that they were), but Focke-Wulf 190s: Germany's most formidable fighters. 'My God, there's at least a dozen of the bastards,' said the flight engineer. I calculated the wind speed and direction, dismantled my Gee-set and installed the G-H receiver. I worked out a series of courses to get us into the target, pulled my parachute from its storage shelf and clipped it onto my chest. I looked out from the astrodome. The Focke-Wulfs were now closing in to attack the hundred Lancasters which flew steadily on.

There must have been an information leak about the raid (the precise target, our numbers, height and time of the attack), which made it possible for German fighters to be ready and waiting for us. The dog-leg courses that we always flew to suggest we were heading for a different target had not deceived them. The *Luftwaffe* knew we were going to the steel works at Witten and the time we should get there. And the Focke-Wulfs were already there in significant force.

The Lancaster just ahead of us was hit by cannon shells and exploded: bombs, fuel, aircraft and seven young men were suddenly a million incandescent fragments in the sky, a huge ball of fire, directly in our path. We flew through it and caught fire. Flames licked along our wings. But the fire had not taken firm hold and began to die down. Lancasters all around us seemed to be performing violent aerobatics, still carrying ten tons of bombs and a heavy load of fuel, to evade fighter attacks. One actually looped-the-loop. A crippled Lancaster with its port wing blown off cartwheeled down the sky alongside us and I saw crew members desperately trying to open escape hatches. I watched the stricken Lancaster's slow movement down the sky: no parachutes opened; no one got out.

'There's a Focke-Wulf on our tail, skipper,' the rear-gunner's flat but unhurried Lancashire voice. 'He hasn't opened fire . . . I'm not going to fire either: he might fire back'. Curiously, the fighter, which turned on us after raking a Lancaster below and behind us with shells, simply flew around with us in his sights, teasing, menacingly, for perhaps six or seven minutes. I waited for what seemed inevitable annihilation high in a cold foreign sky. Perhaps the Focke-Wulf had run out of ammunition. In any event, after what seemed an age, it simply turned and dropped steeply away.

The rear-gunner knew that in straight combat with a Focke-Wulf 190 we had no chance of survival. Heroics, or indeed simply doing his job, would be a suicidal and provocative gesture: we could not possibly win. (A nineteen-year old might have reacted differently, not out of courage but panic, with fatal results.) The armament we carried was pathetically inadequate against a 1944 German fighter. And we all knew it.

In fact, air-gunners were obsolete. They should have been long redundant and their turrets removed, making the Lancaster lighter, more streamlined, adding around 50 mph to its speed. But tradition prevailed. Even the American Flying Fortresses, with their formidable armaments and five gunners, could not adequately repel German fighters. The two great daylight raids on Schweinfurt in August and October 1943 made this abundantly clear: on both raids sixty Fortresses were destroyed by fighters – around 20 per cent of the attacking force. This was an unsustainable rate of loss. The development of long-range American fighters, the Mustangs and Thunderbolts, to accompany the bombers made the Eighth Air Force's future deep-penetration raids less costly. Yet, in the following year a daylight attack on Berlin (6 March 1944) saw sixty-nine American bombers destroyed out of 700, mainly by Focke-Wulf 190s.

The bomber versus the fighter in the Second World War was simply no contest: the only sensible course of action was, if possible, to cut and run. On 12 December 1944 we did not cut and run. And we appeared, in the heat and frenzy of a fast-moving battle, to be losing a lot of Lancasters. In fact, we lost eight, not quite as many as it seemed. We were not, however, a great air armada, but a comparatively small force. In the desperate encounters between bombers and fighters above Witten not a single fighter was shot down.

My survival over Homberg on 21 November was, I believe, a miracle, and since then I have believed in a God. An agnostic or perhaps an atheist before this date, I have been an absolute and unwavering believer ever since. As previously mentioned at Homberg we were flying at about 240 mph; bombs were in free fall from a Lancaster traveling at the same speed directly above us, and yet we escaped almost unscathed. For this cluster of huge bombs simply to straddle us without fatal damage is beyond any simple attribution to 'chance'. A massive blockbuster fell on one side of the fuselage, between the tailplane and the wing. Another, released a few seconds later, fell on the other side of the fuselage, again between the tailplane and wing. A third, on a trajectory that was leading unswervingly to the rear-gunner, missed him by a foot, hit the tailplane but failed to explode, and took a huge slice of the tailplane away. I watched all this, apparently taking place in slow motion, outside time, transfixed, from my astrodome. I cannot begin to imagine the nature of the God in which I now absolutely believe, except that

He is an interventionist, at a personal level, in human affairs. Why, for what purpose, I cannot begin to understand. But I know, without any shadow of doubt, that this is so. On 12 December, when the Focke-Wulf did not attack, was a second miracle (perhaps only a minor one). Two miracles in less than a month. The God who intervened in my life, and the lives of six others over Homberg and Witten is utterly unfathomable, inscrutable. I simply knew that He is.

CHAPTER EIGHT

Fear and Statistics

The losses of Bomber Command were highly publicised. They were an important statement to the world of Britain's unwavering resolve. The death rate among bomber crews had to be high for two principal reasons: to give the message of resolve its maximum impact, and to give moral credibility to the bombers' war. If crews were killing German civilians, it was at the price of grievous loss to themselves. A seriously high death rate in Bomber Command was not simply the inevitable outcome of modern war in the air: it was a moral necessity. It was irrelevant to the moral equation that bombers were not fighting civilians but the uniformed combatants who manned the flak batteries, searchlights, fighter aircraft and radar stations; and that this was a battle that they frequently lost.

There was no other body of fighting men so exposed to the statistics of death. Daily BBC bulletins and Germany's English-language radio broadcasts (which greatly overstated our losses) provided men in training and on the squadrons with a constant diet of aircrew mortality. In the course of the war more than 47,000 men in Bomber Command were killed in action, 8,000 were killed in flying accidents, another 10,000 baled out and became prisoners-of-war, and 8,000 were seriously wounded: 73,000 casualties among 100,000 or so men who flew over a period of six years with Bomber Command. A 73 per cent casualty rate is, by historical standards, extraordinarily high for any military campaign; in fact, 15 per cent might be considered 'normal'. (Short, sharp actions and battles, by contrast with longer-term campaigns, can sometimes experience very high rates of death and overall casualties; although it is perhaps worth noting that the famous 'Charge of the Light Brigade' of the Crimean War, often seen as the supreme example of whole-sale if gallant slaughter, saw 113 men killed out of 673: 16.8 per cent.) In any one night anything from fifty to 500 men of Bomber Command might be killed (on one occasion it was nearly 700); and this proceeded remorselessly by the night, by the week, by the year.

Bomber crews referred to the death toll as the 'chop rate'; and highly publicised statistics – as for no other military campaign – meant it was never far from their minds. (Even high-profile spectaculars like the Army's Dieppe raid in 1942 were subject to no such public statistical dissection.) Death pervaded their lives through long years of training and then squadron service. The statistics of aircrew mortality chipped away at their courage long before they could become airborne over the Third Reich.

It was not only the highly publicised and deeply corrosive statistics that chipped away at a man's store of courage (which I believe is a finite commodity and not easily, or perhaps ever, replenished): it was events. For men on the same course of training or serving on the same squadron, 'events' could differ enormously. War in the dark with a few hundred other invisible bombers in a 'bomber stream' perhaps sixty or seventy miles long and ten miles wide could mean something quite different at the head and the tail. In any event, for some crews bombing missions seemed always to be 'a piece of cake' (until the night they didn't return); their section of sky was always without high drama or significant incident. Their courage remained intact. Other crews were constantly in difficulty, limping home in crippled aircraft with the bomb-aimer wounded and the rear-gunner dead. Their store of courage visibly diminished by the day; and it was a measure of their extraordinary bravery that they finished a tour.

War tends to make cowards of us all – at least, all those (actu-ally a very small minority of servicemen) who experience it at the 'sharp end'. I began my war bravely; my courage steadily declined. I was far less courageous when the war ended than when it began. The level of courage I enjoyed in 1941 has never been regained. Non-combatants will end the war with rather more courage than when it began.

Our constant exposure to the highly publicised statistics of

This emotive image of a Lancaster setting forth on a raid into the night skies of Europe captures the isolation and vulnerability that the crews felt as the late evening light passed into darkness. *(Philip Jarrett)*

Over the target on a daylight raid. High above the clouds this Lancaster delivers Bomber Command's message to Hitler's Nazi regime. *(Philip Jarrett)*

A Lancaster can be seen flying from right to left at the top of this photograph which was taken above the smoke and mayhem caused by a daylight carpet-bombing raid.

(Philip Jarrett)

A bomb-aimer's view of the devastation below. Note the aircraft flying at a lower altitude in the lower part of this photograph. *(Philip Jarrett)*

This photograph was taken by an RAF cameraman during a heavy bomber raid on Magdeburg during an operation on the night of 21 January 1944. A 4,000 pound bomb can be seen plunging towards the target in the centre and towards the top of this remarkable photograph.

(Philip Jarrett)

Explosions light the night sky over Germany in 1944.   *(Philip Jarrett)*

A Lancaster overflying a burning oil depot near Bordeaux during its bombing run.
(Philip Jarrett)

The mighty Krupp factory at Essen after a raid in 1945. *(Philip Jarrett)*

Cologne suffered mightily at the hands of the Allied bombing campaign during the last months of the war. *(Philip Jarrett)*

Bomb damage to
Coblenz.

(Philip Jarrett)

The former capital
of Western
Germany, Bonn, in
1945.

(Philip Jarrett)

Frank Musgrove muses with his pipe. It took him over half a century to rationalise his memories of wartime service that you read between these pages.

The trusty steed.

(Philip Jarrett)

death was mitigated, indeed made tolerable, by one simple fact: it was fragmented and filtered at squadron level to manageable proportions. If thirty aircraft were lost in one night, an actual majority of the forty of fifty squadrons that took part in the raid would actually have lost none.

On the squadron no one put up a notice or otherwise announced who was missing. After debriefing we had gone thankfully to bed; other crews were already there; some had not yet returned. When a crew did not appear at breakfast, unless you knew them quite well, it might be assumed that they had gone on leave or were 'tour-expired'. Whether they were presumed dead in the rubble of Mannheim you wouldn't enquire. Death in Bomber Command was lonely, largely invisible. Losses at squadron level were experienced sporadically, by dribs and drabs.

Max Hastings concludes (in his book, *Bomber Command*) that about 1 per cent of those who flew with the Command were removed (or removed themselves) from flying duties because they had become LMF (Lacking in Moral Fibre). That amounts to about a thousand men over the six years of war. It is difficult to evaluate this statistic. (Set against the Command's 73,000 casualties it seems very small.) But there were lesser degrees of faltering in one's duty than LMF: 'bombing short' was one (very common on the great Berlin raids), and 'early returns' another. About 7 per cent of the bombers that set off for Germany on any particular night turned back early, usually because they claimed to have discovered a serious technical fault. On the great Nuremberg raid at the end of March 1944, for example, 782 heavy bombers were dispatched and fifty-two (6.9 per cent) returned early.

There was usually a suspicion that the technical problem had been 'fixed' to provide a plausible excuse for aborting the mission. The pilot and flight engineer were best placed to arrange such technical problems; the navigator would have much more difficulty in furnishing an excuse. Even malfunctioning Gee-sets and APIs did not make a mission utterly impossible, although certainly very difficult. The bomb-aimer, gunners and signaller had virtually no leverage at all. A defective bomb-sight wouldn't prevent our dropping bombs, albeit not very accurately. Malfunctioning guns would be no excuse at all: they were virtually never used and were of severely limited effectiveness when they were. The signaller never signalled: he observed 'radio silence' in case he gave our position away. He listened in and received signals – perhaps updated information about the winds, perhaps instructions to divert to another airfield on return or even to abort the mission. His inability to receive such messages was scarcely a reason for turning back. 'Early return' decisions were in practice made by the pilot and flight engineer who was to all intents and purposes a second pilot. He helped with the controls and take-off and landing and throughout the flight managed the complex system of fuel supply.

We made two early returns: one was after we were struck by lightning soon after take-off for a raid on Leipzig. The damage to the aircraft's instruments and controls was so extensive that it was quite impossible to proceed and very difficult even to remain airborne.

The second early return was a less clear-cut case. We had a temporary replacement flight engineer who was clearly very reluctant to go with us to Hohenbudberg. Soon after take-off he was reporting to the pilot some trouble with the port-outer engine. Ten minutes later he said it would have to be feathered (that is, the engine turned off). We were now flying on three engines and could probably continue; but then the flight engineer reported problems with the starboard-inner engine and said that would have to be feathered too. This was done, but we clearly could not complete the mission with two engines out of action. We returned to base. To be killed with your own crew was certainly a misfortune; but to be killed with someone else's is sheer stupidity. Our replacement flight engineer was not a stupid man and had no intention of dying with people he scarcely knew.

A bomber squadron had none of the rituals and structural supports that have traditionally aided morale. There was not even the ritual of parades which might assist a sense of community and group solidarity. There was never a parade when I was on the squadron, not even a church parade. There was no swagger or swank; no flags, standards, bugles or drums. Martial music to stir the blood was reserved for the soundtracks of post-war dam-busting films. We set off for battle in clumsy flying gear in an old bus or covered lorry that took us out to the aircraft at their dispersal points. There were no commanders who led from the front. In fact, commanders, even if they were there, were invisible and never issued commands. How could we possibly see their aircraft at night or, without structured formations, even by day? We could neither see them nor hear them by day or by night. Were they actually there?

I was never a commander. However, as a senior NCO and as a commissioned officer, I never gave an order and never received one. The crucial 'order' was the impersonal, printed Battle Order that appeared discreetly, unannounced, on the notice board. Of course, there were infringements of normally courteous behaviour (including respect for rank) that could be admonished or more severely penalised; and at briefing we received instructions about the tracks we must follow and the times we must keep. Even these orders had come down from Command headquarters. The only decision of any importance at squadron level was which of the available crews should be sent on the raid.

Max Hastings makes much of the importance of leadership for aircrew morale: 'The decisive factor in the morale of bomber crews, like that of all fighting men, was leadership.' This is Public School nonsense. John Terraine, in his outstanding book, *The Right of the Line* (1985), shows a far more intelligent grasp of the subtle realities of flying and of squadron life. However elevated his rank, 'who did a rear-gunner ever lead or command?' The same goes for signallers, navigators, bomb-aimers, flight engineers and even pilots. I never knew Johnny issue an order. To do what? He advised us not to bale out when we were struck by lightning. He did not order the rear-gunner to fire (or not to fire) on the Focke-Wulf 190 moving in to attack us on the Witten raid, and I am quite sure that it would never have occurred to him to do so. He asked me (sometimes impatiently) for a course to fly or an ETA especially over the target; but there was really nothing he could 'command' me to do. A squadron was more like a peace-time airport than an Army regiment. It has often struck me how Army officers – even quite junior ones

– talk about 'my men'. RAF officers never talk about 'my men' for the simple reason that they haven't got any.

The squadron had a CO, in rank a wing commander. It also had flight commanders, a navigation leader, a bomb-aimer leader and so on. There was certainly a formal structure of command. But its function was minor administration, virtually invisible: it was certainly not inspirational. The wing commander would usually appear at briefing and say a few words about the target. Was he even going himself? We neither knew nor cared.

At briefing we were not sent off into battle with a stirring oration like that of Henry V before Agincourt. At the most, we had a 'Good Luck, chaps' from the CO (who probably wasn't going anyway). The station commander, a group captain (the equivalent of a full colonel), might be present and say a few words, but he certainly wasn't going: he wasn't even aircrew.

A wing commander who insisted on showing leadership was a serious liability. At one point we had a wing commander who was a decorated air-gunner – a very unusual commanding officer in Bomber Command. He clearly felt that he must lead: but what should he do? There was certainly no possible way in which he could lead from his turret once in the air. He put on a programme of talks that covered discipline and safety in flight – making sure we knew where the various escape hatches were, where the inflatable dinghy was stored, keeping our parachute harness suitably tight so that we didn't slip out of it when we baled out, and procedures to follow in various emergencies. He was killed shortly after running this course when his aircraft, badly damaged over Germany, ditched in the English Channel. The aircraft sank; none of the crew got out.

Our navigation leader didn't, as far as I could see, do much leading either. Nor did he – or could he – 'set an example'. What would he actually do? We did not, like the Americans, fly in formation with the navigator of the lead aircraft taking charge of the route. On the evening we were going to Essen the navigation leader and his crew (his pilot was a flight commander) reached their Lancaster in the gathering dusk. But as he climbed up the ladder into the aircraft he dropped his 'goon bag' – the big green canvas bag in which all navigators carried their maps and charts, preflight calculations and plans, dividers and protractors. The maps, log and charts blew across the airfield and were unlikely to be collected in time for the flight to take place. The flight commander and the navigation leader would not, after all, be going to Essen. We smiled wryly. It might have happened to anyone. Mightn't it? Did it really matter? Would his leadership be missed? We shouldn't even notice that he wasn't there.

Did our commanders lead by example into dangers the crews might not otherwise face? I doubt it. If they did, we might expect them to be killed a little more often. In fact, certainly on my squadron, they were killed rather less. Like all Main Force squadrons that flew throughout the war mine lost 900 men killed. At any given moment there would be on average about 100 men on the squadron (fewer than that in the early years, when the aircraft had a smaller crew, rather more later on). There was one wing commander. If 900 men were killed, we might expect that over a six-year period nine wing commanders would also be killed. However, wing commanders flew a tour of only fifteen missions, so perhaps only four or five should have been killed. But through the entire course of the war only two wing commanders were killed: one in the summer of 1942 and the second more than two years later. Perhaps they were simply better fliers than the rest of us? This, in the broad currents of war, is, I believe, irrelevant. At least four wing commanders should in theory have been killed. However, not only did they fly a short tour, they picked their own targets and crews.

'Leadership' in Bomber Command, from top to bottom, was largely invisible. Our Commander-in-Chief, the great Butcher Harris, was the most invisible of them all in his headquarters at High Wycombe. He certainly cannot be accused of leading from the front. He never flew – he did not go on a single Bomber Command raid. He very seldom visited a bomber station. (I never saw him and knew no one who had.) He was not 'Bomber Harris', he was 'Butcher Harris'; and he was Butcher Harris not because he butchered Germans but because he butchered his crews. Curiously, this earned him our highest regard: his sheer cussedness, ruthlessness and barbarity made him one 'non-operational bastard' whom we could actually respect.

It is remarkable that morale should have held up so well in the highly fluid, unstructured relationships of squadron life. Crews were constantly joining the squadron, leaving it after nine or ten months when they had completed their tour, or failing to return from 'ops'. All was instability and flux. A squadron was less like a family, college or club than a railway station: there were constant arrivals and departures and brief encounters. Squadrons did not have names (although a few had a name referring to some imperial connection in brackets): they had numbers. Unlike many Army regiments, they were not redolent of personality and place. Even their numbers followed no sequence that made any obvious sense. In the nature of things they had no battle honours stretching back to the Peninsular War: they had to make the most of a posthumous Victoria Cross.

The men of Bomber Command appeared to experience all the arbitrariness, the transience and the accident of war. The variety of experience between squadrons and even within squadrons was enormous, underscoring the apparently fortuitous nature of an aerial combatant's life. On any particular bombing mission the experience and loss rates of the squadrons taking part were highly diverse. Thus, on the Nuremberg raid in March 1944, when ninety-five aircraft were lost and forty squadrons took part, 420 Squadron at Tholthorpe dispatched fourteen Halifaxes and lost none; 626 Squadron at Wickenby sent sixteen Lancasters and lost none; 100 Squadron at Grimsby sent eighteen Lancasters and lost none; but 51 Squadron at Snaith sent seventeen Halifaxes and lost five; and 101 Squadron at Ludford Magna sent twenty-six Lancasters and lost six. This pattern makes no kind of sense.

Yet, the bombers' war was defined by public statistics and aircrews were deeply impregnated by frequencies and statistical trends. It is true that BBC statistics were usually crude numbers, seldom offering the refinement of percentages. Beneath the flux of numbers, however, there was an underlying orderliness, ineluctable structures and regularities of which one became intuitively aware.

The first great uniformity is the fact (not of course known at the time) of 900 deaths per Main Force squadron throughout the course of the war – plus or minus about 5 per cent. Despite the great variations in squadron fortunes on any particular night, over six years their fortunes were virtually the same – although they had flown different kinds of aircraft to different targets (albeit with a good deal of overlap, from airfields in a wide range of locations throughout eastern England. For comparative purposes a standardised measure is commonly used: squadron losses are stated as a ratio of aircraft lost to sorties flown; and it is invariably about 3.0 per cent. No. 44 Squadron in Lincolnshire flew Hampdens then Lancasters on 6405 sorties; 192 aircraft were lost, a ratio of 3.0 per cent. No. 15 Squadron in Norfolk flew Blenheims, Battles, Wellingtons, Stirlings and Lancasters on 5787 sorties; 166 aircraft were lost, a ratio of 2.9 per cent. Whatever the vagaries of war as experienced this week or that, inexorably over a six-year period the ratio of aircraft lost to sorties flown would be 3 per cent. This is a basic structural feature of the bombers' war. Nine hundred men who served on a squadron would be killed. This was the mathematical certainty from which the young men who flew the bombers had no chance of escape.

This highly mathematical-statistical war in the air left anyone flying with Bomber Command with a profound sense of averages: and if others were keeping up the averages, it was less likely to be you. And so a healthy rate of men killed was your greatest hope. Likewise with aircraft coned over a target: when the searchlights settled on someone else, you could relax: they'd got some other poor bastard; you were probably safe.

In this curious war of surface flux and deep underlying regularities and structures – a war which proceeded at two different speeds – young men struggled to survive. Their morale was not sustained to any significant degree by leadership or by reassuring rituals: the concept of a 'tour' was an inspired 'structural' invention which sustained most crews (but a requirement of more than thirty missions, say forty-five or fifty, would have found very few aircrew volunteers). With a target of thirty, a crew simply got on with it. In battle they were entirely alone. They were leaderless men. At night we saw no aircraft from take-off to landing: we kept radio silence; on Main Force raids the only 'order' we heard was the Master Bomber directing us to particular clusters of flares. Even in daylight we had no leaders: we did not fly in formation with a leader at our head.

Over the target we were a rabble, a mêlée, a scrum.

In spite of the 'early returns' and the small minority of crewmen who went LMF, what I recall most vividly and with pride, and see as typical or Bomber Command, is the daylight mission I flew to Witten on 12 December 1944. It was a routine affair of no particular note. For more than half an hour before the target we knew that we should encounter head-on, ready and waiting, the world's most formidable fighters, Focke-Wulf 190s. This was certainly not the Charge of the Light Brigade with a Lord Cardigan leading from the front. Nobody was leading from the front. In fact, nobody was leading at all. It was as usual each crew for itself. But no aircraft faltered. While there was still ample time, nobody dropped back perhaps to divert to a different target. All flew on towards a contest in which no bomber versus a fighter could possibly prevail. I am sure it never occurred to anyone to do otherwise. Shortly fifty-six men would die in the cold skies four miles above the Ruhrstahl steel-works in north Germany. It was an unremarkable battle in the annals of war; after all, only half as many were killed as in the Charge of the Light Brigade from the same number of men.

The real trouble is, that you know you've got to go and do it again . . . and again . . . and again.

What manner of men were these? Who were the extraordinary young men who flew with Bomber Command? By 1944 they were not, except in tiny numbers, pre-war professionals, even in a squadron's senior ranks. Everyone was a volunteer. They were mostly born within a narrow span of ten years or so, between 1912 and 1922: the oldest would be around twenty-seven when the war began, the youngest (like me) about seventeen. They were rigorously tested by the RAF, but they were all in the first instance self-selected; they were no doubt 'inner-directed', too. They were of high intelligence and in very good physical shape. (They were very good looking men.) In fact they were, for the most part, the eleven-plus scholarship boys, the 10 or 12 per cent of their age group who had passed their exams and entered the state secondary grammar schools. They were diligent, highly conscientious, inwardly motivated; they could be relied upon to do their homework and were seldom a 'discipline problem'. They did what their teachers told them and got their Matric,

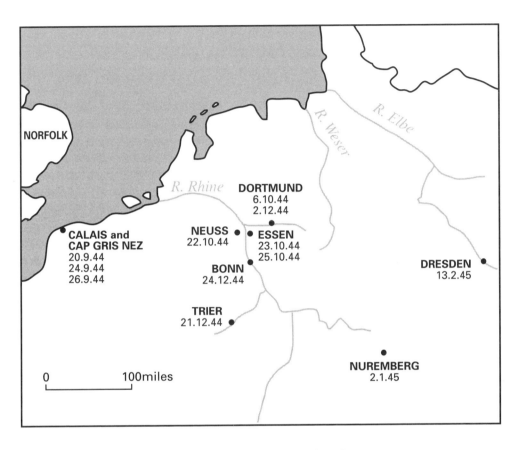

'MAIN FORCE' TARGETS
(German troop concentrations and industrial centres)

Higher School Certificate, and often their honours degree. They were a new twentieth-century meritocratic elite, the product of a first-rate system of secondary school education, humane and broadly based, which rejected all methods of 'force-feeding'. It had been developed since the Balfour Education Act of 1902, reached its high point in the interwar years, and is now to our detriment extinct.

The former pupils of the secondary grammar schools, with

their Matric and perhaps HSC, rose magnificently, at times hero-
ically, to their country's challenge. The challenge called for great
technical skill and quick intelligence as well as high courage. As
pilots and navigators they were tailor-made for the job. They
were often afraid and reluctant to carry on, but the vast majority
did. They did not need leaders and formal structures. They
simply got on with it.

The Master Bomber was no more than a traffic policeman –
rather less, because there were no sanctions he could possibly
apply to those, say, who might be 'bombing short'. The only
'discipline' was the track laid down for us to follow and the
airborne camera that automatically photographed the target we
had actually bombed. I suppose we might have gone nowhere
near the designated target and flown for a time to somewhere
relatively safe. (Where in any case was safe?) But camera or no
camera, I don't think it ever occurred to us to do that – although
some crews did actually fly to neutral Sweden and Switzerland
(perhaps because they had technical problems) – and found
safety for the rest of the war.

CHAPTER NINE

Dresden

By the end of 1944 I had almost completed my tour. For me this was a time of particular tension. During the first twenty or so missions you live in the present, you don't look far ahead. Completing a tour seems a long way away, and you may not actually get there. But, somewhat surprised, you find that you have completed twenty-four or twenty-five missions. You take stock: 'I've got this far and might after all make it.' But stories of crews who failed to return from their twenty-eighth, twenty-ninth or thirtieth mission abounded in Bomber Command. They were told with some relish. Experience was no protection. It seemed somehow to add to the risk.

The year 1945 did not begin auspiciously for the Allied war effort in Europe. For the bomber squadrons there was no sense of imminent victory, only of crisis. The mood had soured after the defeat of our airborne army at Arnhem in the previous September; and the German Ardennes offensive in December, when the Allies were all but pushed back into the sea, showed how precariously our forward positions were held. The British Army was making slow progress and had not yet crossed the Rhine – and in fact would not do so until 25 March. The attacks on London and southern England by V1 rockets and pilotless flying bombs were causing grave concern: 9000 Londoners were killed in a campaign of cowardice involving no risk whatsoever to German lives. Winston Churchill was desperate and even considered the use of poison gas ('mainly mustard') as the only effective retaliation; or the systematic destruction of twelve named German cities by Bomber Command. Victory in the west seemed to be receding. At a meeting of the War Cabinet on 12

January it was estimated that the war in Europe could not be concluded until at least December 1945.

The New Year began ominously for Bomber Command. On 5 January an attack was made on Hanover with thirty-one heavy bombers lost, some 5 per cent of the total force. On 14 January a long-range attack on oil refineries near Leipzig saw the loss of ten more aircraft. In the first three months of 1945, 521 heavy bombers were lost, more than in the first three months of 1943 (376 lost), although fewer than in 1944 (766), which saw the climax of the Berlin raids. My crew did not appear on the Battle Order until 13 February. The target that night was Dresden.

A steadily rising proportion of bombing missions was being flown against distant targets in eastern Germany, involving a flying time of around nine or ten hours. Oil refineries in particular were coming under attack, often with grievous aircrew losses. This was four years after an Air Ministry directive had been sent to Sir Richard Peirse, the then Chief of Bomber Command, highlighting the overriding importance of oil plants in his bombing campaign. More than a dozen sites were listed, including Magdeburg and Gelsenkirchen, but some were near the far-eastern frontier of Germany, including Leuna, Pölitz, Böhlen and Lutzkendorf. Peirse's campaign against the oil targets achieved nothing and was abandoned after a month. Four years later the eastern oil plants had assumed a still greater significance: they were vital to Germany's defence against the Russian advance. Bomber Command turned to these targets again but now with telling effect, although the bomber losses were high. An attack on refineries near Stettin in February (when twelve Lancasters were lost) was counted as a particularly notable success.

Leuna was attacked on 14 January with ten Lancasters lost; Pölitz was attacked on 8 February with twelve lost; Rositz near Leipzig was attacked on 14 February when four were lost; Böhlen near Dresden was the target on 20 March for the loss of nine; but eighteen Lancasters were lost (7.4 per cent of the force) in an attack on Lutzkendorf on 4 April. Regensburg, attacked on 20 April, was the most distant of these targets. Sixty Lancasters were lost attacking these six 'far-eastern' oil targets in the early months of 1945.

The eastern front was claiming the lives of a steeply rising number of England's finest young men. Operation *Thunderclap* had been launched by the RAF in January specifically to help the Russian advance into eastern Germany. On 4 February, at the Yalta Conference of the Allied leaders, Stalin asked for attacks of this kind to be intensified. As a direct consequence, the Air Ministry, with Churchill's knowledge and encouragement, asked Bomber Command to carry out heavy raids on Leipzig, Chemnitz and Dresden. The attack on Dresden was part of a wider plan instigated by the very highest authority.

On the morning of 13 February my crew was on the Battle Order. This would be my last operational flight. I was greatly relieved: now, one way or another, I would finish my tour. The usual speculation about the possible target was rife throughout the day. Clearly it was a 'far-eastern' target: there was a heavy fuel load and a light bomb load with a large component of incendiaries. Perhaps it would be Nuremburg, Leipzig or even Berlin. No one even suggested Dresden.

However, at 6 o'clock when the crews assembled for the main briefing, no one was particularly surprised. Certainly no one was shocked when the target was at last revealed. I had flown bombing missions to Essen, Dortmund, Cologne and Nuremburg: Dresden was just another major industrial city scheduled for attack, with the added urgency that it was now, apparently, impeding the Red Army's advance. The briefing officer made it crystal clear that this attack was one that the Russians particularly wanted; we understood that Dresden was an important communication centre and assembly point for German troops destined for a crucial sector of the eastern front. No one walked out and refused to go. I am quite sure that it never occurred to anyone among these hundred well educated men to do so. There was no muttering among crews about the impropriety of the target as we collected our escape kits and parachutes and climbed into the bus that took us out to the Lancasters. The ground crews knew where we were going: they didn't refuse to prepare the Lancasters for their mission. In any event they'd be back in the NAAFI; they wouldn't be carrying the bombs.

I knew that Dresden was famous for china, just as I knew that my home town, Nottingham, was famous for lace. But I did not connect these facts. I did not think: 'This will repay the bombing of the lace market.' That was utterly irrelevant. The Germans were the enemy, still a formidable and quite ruthless foe; we were in the business of defeating Hitler's Reich.

My principal concern on 13 February was the distance. I knew it would be a clear night. A great air armada would rise out of eastern England and fly to the distant extremities of Germany: a great feat of arms; a ten-hour battle in the skies; no less remarkable for being almost routine. I was proud to be part of it. I thought: 'We shall lose twenty Lancasters tonight.' I felt I had been dealt a rather poor hand for the last flight of my tour. (In the event we lost only nine Lancasters.)

We took off from Norfolk at ten minutes to ten. It was nearly ten hours later that we got back, exhausted, but relieved, to a breakfast of ham and eggs.

The flight to Dresden through a cloudless night went surprisingly well. While we were in Gee range I obtained fixes every twenty minutes and calculated the wind. It was reassuringly constant: 50 mph from 300 degrees at 20,000 feet. The meteorological forecast had not indicated any frontal system through which we would fly, with consequent major changes in wind speed and direction. I changed course on my ETA at turning points with confidence in the calculations I had made. Some four hours later, exactly on cue, we saw a blazing target ahead, marked with the Path Finders' flares, now clearly under heavy attack alongside the silver ribbon of the Elbe.

The defences were light. Searchlights were few, groping and uncertain; flak appeared to be erratic. There was no indication of fighter activity. The Master Bomber directed the Lancasters to attack new clusters of flares. The ground 20,000 feet below was spectacular, vivid with explosions – a tremendous and terrible pyrotechnic display. We made our bombing run steadily, uneventfully, and turned thankfully for home. The rear-gunner sat facing the firestorm and could see it clearly for the next two hours.

We landed safely in Norfolk. My feelings were of immense relief. Nearly four years after my interview with a young RAF officer at my Nottingham grammar school my personal mission was now complete. I had finished my tour. It had been an arduous and dangerous four years, full of excitement and fear. I had not performed particularly well, but I had done it. I had survived. With hindsight and in the full glare of history Dresden was hardly the Holy Grail, but for me, a pilgrimage, indeed a crusade, was complete.

What do I think now, nearly sixty years on? I have not the slightest regret for having flown to Dresden on that clear night

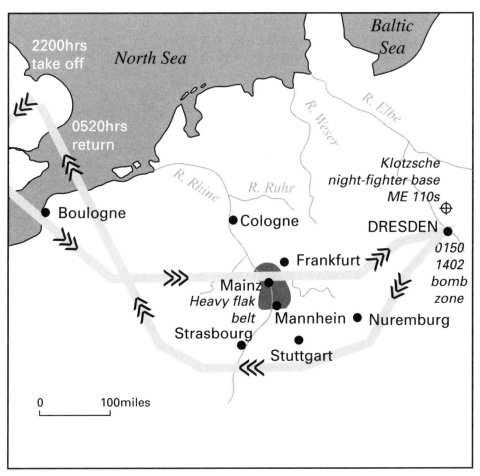

DRESDEN: 13/14 FEBRUARY 1945
(2200hrs 13 February – 0520hrs 14 February)

in February 1945, hardly daring to hope that I would return. But I am filled with bitterness at the loss of more than 700 of England's finest young men in the 'far-eastern' bombing campaign of which Dresden was merely a part. It extended for three months from mid-January to mid-April 1945. This was Churchillian gesture-politics at its worst: a futile attempt to rebut Stalin's constant contemptuous charge that the English people were cowards, leaving the brunt of the fighting and the greatest sacrifice to the Soviet Union. More than 700 men were sacrificed to make a point. Apart from the six oil targets that Bomber Command attacked for the loss of sixty aircraft and 420 men, four non-oil targets were attacked for the loss of fifty-one aircraft and 357 men. Chemnitz was attacked twice, with thirty-four aircraft lost; an attack on Leipzig on 10 April by seventy bombers resulted in a loss of 10 per cent. In the three months of the air battle of eastern Europe we lost 780 men and facilitated the Red Army's savage advance to Berlin.

This is my regret about Dresden: that it helped the Russians establish themselves deep inside Europe with appalling ferocity, and prevented the very balance of power that we had fought to restore.

When we had finished our tour the crew dispersed; we were posted from the squadron and went our separate ways. We never met again. Johnny the pilot and Jack the bomb-aimer both returned to Australia. They sent me food parcels for a number of years after the war when they thought I was starving.

I was posted as a lecturer in air navigation to an OTU at Silverstone, the famous present-day racing course. This period was, I think, the happiest in my life. The relief from the tension of a front-line squadron was enormous. I enjoyed presenting some of the problems of air navigation 'at the sharp end' of war and explaining some of the solutions. Once a week I flew on a night 'cross-country' exercise with a trainee crew in an ancient Wellington bomber. This was not without risk, and my job of helping the trainee navigator out of any difficulties he encountered was almost pointless. The speed of flight makes recovery very difficult. If a trainee navigator has, quite literally, 'lost the plot', events are moving too rapidly for anyone to take over and sort the problem out quickly. You will be lost for an uncomfortable long time, until you have obtained new fixes, calculated new winds, and worked out new courses to fly and revised ETAs. Hopefully, you have not hit a peak in the Cairngorms in the meantime.

But this was nice . . . I was useful, putting my experience to some purpose, respected by my well motivated students (they wished to survive), and mercifully relaxed. When the Lancasters were taking off for Germany I was enjoying skittles in Northamptonshire's village pubs. Life has never been quite so good again.

CHAPTER TEN

Retrospect

I was very proud to be selected for flying duties with RAF Bomber Command. Sixty years later I am still proud to have served as a navigator on heavy bombers, albeit not one of any particular distinction. The very ordinariness of my long period of training and subsequent experience of aerial combat may make this story worth telling.

In later life I enjoyed an academic career of some note. I published a number of well received books, was appointed to university professorships at home and abroad, and achieved an international reputation in my particular field; but my period with Bomber Command remains the most important time of my life.

It is curious, therefore, that for fifty years after the war I found it very difficult to talk about my wartime experiences and almost never did so. It is only quite recently that I have felt able to mention these long-past events and this memoir is a product of this belated sense of release. I worked with colleagues for years and lived alongside neighbours who probably thought, if they thought about it at all, that I had never experienced military service. I do not have the appearance and bearing of a military man. I never mentioned this episode in my life even to closest friends. I am not entirely sure now why I was so reticent. Perhaps I was afraid of being a bore and seeming guilty of 'shooting a line'; perhaps I thought that my contribution did not rate very high alongside the well publi-cised stories of numerous wartime heroes. And of course it does not. It is an ordinary story of an ordinary young man caught up in extraordinary events.

I have certainly gained nothing whatsoever in any material

sense from my RAF service. My education was seriously disrupted and my career plans undermined. I soon found, when I was applying for jobs after the war (in the educational sphere), that I was seen as someone closely akin to a war criminal. 'What did you think about the women and children below when you were dropping your bombs?' Any mention of my being at Dresden, and I might as well not have applied. I was branded for life. I omitted all details of my war record from my curriculum vitae and simply noted, 'Served with the Royal Air Force 1941–5.' As a (presumed) member of the ground staff who had stayed well clear of combatant duties and had kept the bombers flying to the great German cities, I knew that I was morally in the clear, wholly beyond reproach.

Was I beyond reproach? What were my motives in wishing to fly with the RAF, and especially with Bomber Command? In conventional psychological terms of personal motivation, it was not, I believe, to satisfy the Id. I was not seeking revenge and the satisfaction of some deeply primitive urge to aggression. It was also not to any serious extent an affair of the Ego: to engage in some personal display and perhaps achieve glory. I would attribute my volunteering in 1941 primarily to the Superego: to an over-conscientiousness. I had in particular a very strong sense of the obligation I owed for my somewhat superior, 'selective', Grammar school education, enjoyed by only a very small minority of my age group. After all, I had my Matric with Distinctions in Physics and Maths.

However, of course, it was much more complicated than that. Here, after all, was the promise of high adventure. I was never greatly inspired by the Battle of Britain; but the hard slog of a night raid on Stettin had a curiously visceral appeal.

It is difficult to understand now, how the bombing war in the early war years was invested with an immense moral authority, especially after the army retreated from Europe in 1940. Not only would it be the principal, if not the only, means of our winning the war, but it would save perhaps a million soldiers' lives. What higher morality could there be? The public men who had fought in the First World War had a palpable horror of repeating the carnage of the trenches. However, for the loss of sixty or seventy thousand lives in the air, perhaps three-quarters of a million would be saved on the ground. It seemed an excellent bargain. This thinking ran through our military strategy and, indeed, through a generalised national understanding, right up to the end. It was also the view that effectively brought America into the war. The lives of these airmen would be a (relatively small) sacrifice that would make large-scale ground operations unnecessary.

In 1944 the squadrons were fully aware of this view. Sometimes I felt some resentment at being a sacrificial lamb while vast sections of the Army, year after year, did virtually nothing. But by now, it was clear the Army would be called upon to make a more significant contribution than was once thought.

The greatest moral authority, as well as the essential intellectual and technical skills, came from the nation's secondary grammar schools. They were virtually incorporated into the aerial war effort at a very early stage through the institution of the ATC (Air Training Corps). Overnight, grammar school headmasters became flight lieutenants and squadron leaders, splendidly uniformed commanding officers of the school corps. Senior physics and mathematics masters became instant flying officers, instructors in elementary air navigation and the principles of flight. I refused to join. It was not obligatory, but fifth and sixth formers were under immense pressure to do so. I was sternly interviewed by the headmaster, my housemaster and my form master for my lack of patriotism. I informed them that this was under-age conscription by the back door (the call-up age was still twenty). It was a school, not a junior military academy, or some Anglicised version of the Hitler Youth. The public schools almost invariably had an Army Corps and were less welcoming to the upstart ATC, but the 1200 or so state grammar schools were being required to underpin the bombers' war effectively by government decree.

Most of the members of the school training corps would not fly, but enter highly skilled ground staff trades especially in radar; but the moral authority of 1200 grammar school headmasters had clearly been enlisted for the RAF's war, including the bombing campaign. None of the headmasters resigned their commissions after the firestorm their former pupils had ignited in Hamburg or even Dresden; none divested themselves of their uniforms and disbanded the school corps.

I have said that I have never gained from my war service in any material sense. In fact, the opposite has been the case; but there were significant non-material gains. I was young and learned a great deal about myself, especially the extent and limits of my courage, which I had considerably over-estimated in 1941. I learned also something of my intellectual limitations (but was pleased I could continue to function quite well under fire). My scarcity-value in 1941, with my Matric in Physics and Maths, I had certainly exaggerated. There seemed to be an endless supply of men of the appropriate age who had these basic attainments, were eager to make use of them in the air, and could do their job at least as well as I could, if not better. Navigation on bombing missions certainly called for quick responses and intellectual improvisation in highly varied and unpredictable conditions. My overriding sense of bombing raids is not the fear of imminent death in a burning and disintegrating Lancaster bomber, but of getting it wrong – the sheer harass-ment of obtaining a fix and a wind. And in the uncertainty and bewilderment of it all thinking: 'What in God's name am I doing here?'

I do not believe that in joining the RAF I was unduly influ-enced by early wartime propaganda that glamorised pilots and war in the air. I was not particularly impressed by films, which found enthusiastic audiences, like *Dangerous Moonlight*, with its thundering Warsaw concerto soundtrack, or even the grossly overacted *First of the Few*. *Target for Tonight*, however, was a different matter. It was a short, low-key, documentary-style film, which I saw at a Nottingham cinema in 1940. It portrayed a night-time mission over Germany by a Wellington bomber. It was cheaply made entirely in the studio, with a serving RAF officer as the pilot (he was killed later, in 1944, flying a Mosquito). There was even a quite realistic portrayal of the observer's (navigator's) problems, and the discomforts of in-habiting a military aircraft designed not to carry people but bombs. I was enthralled. This, I thought, is what I should really like to do. A year or two later I myself flew as the navigator of many Wellington bombers; and all of them were touched a little with the magic of the mock-up F for Freddie in *Target for Tonight*. I can smell their distinctive warm cosiness infused with petrol fumes and resin even now.

More potent even than *Target for Tonight* was the actual bombing raid on Augsburg on 17 April 1942. (By now I was well established on my initial aircrew training course and had done some flying, curiously, on patrol with a Polish squadron flying Beaufighters from Middle Wallop.) The Augsburg raid was a brilliant and well publicised spectacular. It was flown at low level, in daylight, deep into Germany. Twelve Lancasters took off from Lincolnshire to attack the submarine diesel factory at Augsburg. It would mean ten hours in the air. They would cross France at chimney-pot height, skirt Switzerland, and reach Augsburg in the late afternoon. Four Lancasters were shot down by German fighters shortly after crossing the French coast. The remaining eight aircraft arrived on cue over Augsburg and flew into a storm of flak. One was hit immediately and went down smoking, crashing in a ball of flame; two more met a similar fate. The remaining five Lancasters made their way home in the gathering dusk. Fifty men out of the eighty who set out would not be coming home.

The effect of this feat of arms was electrifying. I was in no way deterred from my chosen path into war, but immeasurably uplifted. The hair on the back of my head stood on end. This was gallantry of the highest order, which I could recognise, but to which I could never hope to aspire.

Such highly dramatic, but relatively small-scale events impinged decisively on my life in my nineteenth year. However, there were much wider issues of which I was fully aware and with which I was deeply concerned. One was the balance of power. I am still deeply concerned about it now.

I did not go to war with any sense of moral outrage against the German people or even the German government. I had seen my hometown dive-bombed by Stukas and part of our English heritage destroyed; I had been in Birmingham when it was under heavy attack from the air; and I had also been in London. But this was war. I was not even outraged by the alleged maltreatment of Germany's minorities (the concentration camps came later and were not fully known in all their awfulness until the war was almost over). No country should go to war for moral reasons; there can be no end to it. I did not volunteer to fight against Germany because I was anti-German; in fact, I was pro-German. My huge admiration for the German people was virtually undimmed. As it still is.

I knew something of Germany's immense contribution to philosophy, science, mathematics, literature and music. I was impressed by the Germans' history of courage and high proficiency in war, but I had no wish to see them dominate the whole of Europe and occupy England. After Germany's invasion of Poland and Czechoslovakia I knew that what was at issue was the European balance of power and that we had no option but to stand and fight.

Like Churchill I was fighting not only for England but Empire. This was part of the balance of power too: it gave us international clout and enabled us, even in Europe, to punch more than our weight. I saw the Empire as a beneficent force: not only in the conduct of international affairs, but in the progress the indigenous people could make. In the 1930s it was my hope to go to Oxford and then take the examinations for the Indian Civil Service, with a preference for a posting to Burma. War stopped all that. Instead of the Empire I joined Bomber Command.

We lost both the Empire and the European balance of power. The entire British Empire was not 'lost' immediately (and in fact I served for a time in the post-war colonial education service in Uganda). However, it was clearly unsustainable, partly because we couldn't afford it, but principally because America disapproved. (We certainly left Africa far too early, and the consequence has been catastrophe.) The balance of power in Europe had been irretrievably lost after our failure at Arnhem in autumn 1944. The Russians would now reach Berlin long before we could; and a grotesque power imbalance within Europe would spell a new barbarism far worse than anything we had set out to overthrow.

For a year in my degree course at Oxford I was a pupil of A.J.P. Taylor. In a notorious book entitled *The Course of German History* (1945) he had proclaimed Churchill's alliance with Russia in 1941 as 'the greatest act of statesmanship of the century'. Taylor had also advocated the permanent disunity of Germany, at least in the sense of its sharp separation from Austria and retreat into the municipal autonomies and small states which had constituted 'Germany' in the past. The historian who claimed to understand power and the importance of its sensible and equitable distribution had completely failed to grasp the enormity of the Russian advance.

I always thought Taylor a historian of shallow intellect, a superficially clever man with a head crammed with 'short-term' facts. He had no sense of longer-term currents and trends, underlying rhythms and deeper structures in history, only surface fluidity and flux. For him, inevitably, history always moved on through a process of muddle. In a year Taylor put me off history for life. I found refuge in sociology. Even when I was a history student, I thought his anti-German history of Germany was a tendentious tract for the times.

His perspective was astonishingly parochial. It is true that his 'parish' was Europe; but he made no effort to look beyond it and place it in context. Europe was no longer simply something in itself. It was now part of a constellation of international power blocks. The Allies, by insisting on the preposterous requirement of Germany's 'unconditional surrender' and dismemberment, had emasculated Europe and destroyed its ability ever to hold its own in the post-war world.

What is at issue now is not the balance of power in Europe, among Taylor's 'Great Powers', but the balance of power in the world. Europe must not see its independence and its ancient and distinctive values and culture eroded by the pervasive influence of any lone and vastly rich Superpower. Since the Crusades, Europe has enjoyed a strong and unifying tradition of chivalry embodied in the Christian knight and his descendant the (largely secularised) 'gentleman', which we must recover and reinterpret for our age. The civilisation of the amoral market must not prevail everywhere. As the economist Joseph Schumpeter observed as he cast a sceptical eye over the future of capitalism: the Stock Exchange is a poor substitute for the Holy Grail.

When I now look back over the past sixty years I weep for the 55,000 men of Bomber Command who have not lived to enjoy

them; and I weep for Europe. Europe has been grievously
enfeebled. Two nations rose immeasurably during and because
of the war: Russia and America. Europe was utterly diminished.

What of the future? Europe can certainly recover its rightful
place among the world's superpowers and in the interest of

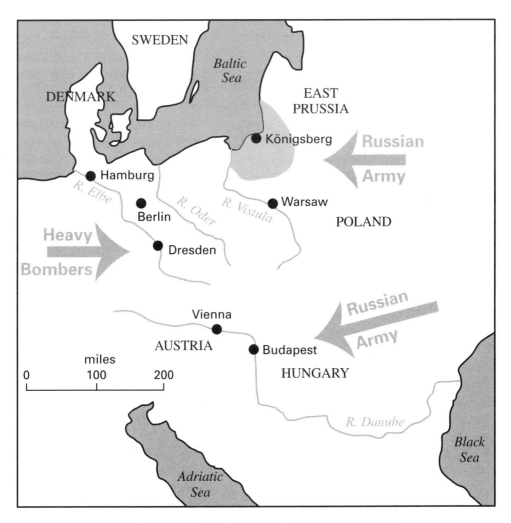

EASTERN PERSPECTIVE: FEBRUARY 1945
Dresden (firestorm) Budapest (massacre) East Prussia
(genocide)

humanity must do so. (But it will have to achieve a degree of genuine integration that at the moment Britain finds un-palatable.) Bomber Command will undoubtedly be reassessed from time to time by the military historians. They may explain why, in recent years, only the Queen Mother, among the nation's leading figures, dared pay public tribute to the late Sir Arthur Harris.

The sheer enormity of Bomber Command's sacrifice has never been properly recognised. A true evaluation calls for very difficult comparative studies. We need to confront some awkward statistics. It might be useful to take a cursory look, for instance, at the battle of E1 Alamein in 1942, where 2350 men were killed. (Even in highly reputable histories this is often stated as 13,560, but this figure is actually for 'casualties' – the wounded and missing as well as the dead.) This total of fatali-ties is rather less than the 2690 Bomber Command aircrew killed in the space of a few months over Berlin at the end of 1943 and early in 1944. The E1 Alamein fatalities occurred in Montgomery's Eighth Army, which numbered 195,000 men; the men killed over Berlin came from a Command that numbered about 8000. Of course, the comparison may be considered wholly invalid because the Eighth Army was a highly complex, polyglot organisation in which many, perhaps a majority, would not be front-line fighting men. Even so, the death rate is astonishingly low for a great battle that allegedly changed the course of the war. (At Waterloo, Wellington lost 14,000 men from a field army of 70,000; Blücher likewise lost 20 per cent killed from a somewhat larger Prussian force – a total loss of 30,000 men.)

Those killed at E1 Alamein constituted 1.5 per cent of Montgomery's Eighth Army; but there are, perhaps, insuperable objections to making this comparison. Arnhem and the Battle of Britain might furnish more satisfactory examples: we are here much nearer to comparing like with like. They were all front-line fighting men. In ten days in September 1944 11,920 British (with some Polish) airborne troops took part in the Battle of Arnhem, of whom 1485 were killed – 12.5 per cent. All the men at Arnhem were certainly in the front line, although some were engineers, medical staff or radio-repair men. Bomber Command in almost six years of war lost 55,000 men killed out of over 100,000 who served at one time or another in the Command: a death rate of roughly 50 per cent. Perhaps, however, this is not a valid comparison either.

In the Battle of Britain in 1940, fought by Fighter Command over a period of some five months in the summer and autumn, around 3000 pilots at one time or another took part. (It is difficult to know by what criterion they have been described as 'the Few'.) From these, 520 were killed – 17 per cent. We are therefore comparing three death rates: Arnhem – 12.5 per cent; the Battle of Britain – 17 per cent; and Bomber Command – 50 per cent. These statistics raise some obvious problems of comparability but are at least worth some careful reflection.

The deaths in Bomber Command were as astonishingly high as those at El Alamein were astonishingly low. (Fighter Command's losses in 1940 were within the range of 'normality' for a major military engagement and are more or less within the same bracket as Arnhem.) Bomber Command's losses were abnormally high by whatever yardstick we use. In the first five months of 1944 the Command was virtually wiped out: the number of men and aircraft lost was equal to the normal strength of the Command. This fact was obscured by the unfailing flow of replacement crews from the training units and of aircraft from the factories.

Yet, modern wartime armies provide a remarkably benign environment for the vast majority of those who serve in them. In the Boer War an army of 440,000 was assembled in South Africa to fight for Great Britain: in nearly three years of war 8000 were killed – 1.8 per cent. (A further 13,000 died of disease – a total fatality rate of 4.8 per cent.) In the First World War, 8.4 per cent of those who put on a uniform to fight for king and country were killed (702,410 out of 8,375,000). This is a war with a reputation for wholesale and mindless slaughter. In the Second World War the rate was scarcely a quarter of this, less than 3 per cent. However, some groups and categories of fighting men may in the course of a war suffer 20 per cent fatalities. As recent research by Gordon Corrigan shows, old Etonians who fought in the First World War experienced such losses (1157 out of 5650). Old Boys of Tonbridge School suffered almost exactly the same rate of fatalities – 19 per cent (415 out of 2225). Similarly Old Sedberghians suffered a death rate of 20 per cent: 251 out of 1250. These were the Public Schools that provided the officer class of elite fighting units. In a similar fashion Oxford and Cambridge graduates provided 17,670 men who fought in the war of whom 3750 (21 per cent) were killed. (These death rates are the same as those in Wellington's army at Waterloo a century before.) Over the past two centuries death rates of 20 per cent are very high for any sector of troops in any campaign or over the course of a war – 50 per cent is extraordinary. The well educated, upper class young men from Public Schools and Oxford and Cambridge who were killed in the First World War are often referred to as 'the lost generation' of England's future leaders, although 80 per cent of them returned home. In my opinion the real 'lost generation' of young men of great ability and promise were those in the Second World War who flew with Bomber Command.

The low overall proportion of fatalities in modern war arises partly because the ratio of support troops (relatively safe) to front-line fighting men is very high – about 80 per cent to 20 per cent. Also, (in the Second World War) most of the armed forces were not actually fighting the enemy for long periods of time – they spent four years waiting for D-Day. The fighting that did occur at this time was in relatively small-scale, peripheral campaigns. (When D-Day came, the Normandy campaign sustained casualties comparable to the Somme nearly thirty years earlier.)

The aircrew of Bomber Command, by contrast, engaged the enemy week after week through nearly six years of war. They were all front-line fighters, although their 'tour' in the front line was limited. If, on average, 5 per cent of men were lost on each raid, after twenty raids (if each was a 'maximum effort') there would be nobody left. In the first five months of 1944, 1286 bombers were missing over Germany, which means 9000 men. (Another 155 aircraft crashed in England.) This is as many aircraft and aircrew as there were at any one time in Bomber Command.

The overall picture of death in the course of the Second World War seems to be: 3 per cent of all men in uniform were killed;

perhaps between 10 and 12 per cent of all front-line land (and sea) forces; and 50 per cent of those who flew the heavy bombers. The difference between the overall 3 per cent and Bomber Command's 50 per cent borders on the grotesque.

CHAPTER ELEVEN

Ius in Bellum

In writing this memoir, the moral issues that surround the bombing campaign have arisen from time to time. They did not concern me greatly in the 1940s but have come to haunt me more insistently as the years have passed. What did I think of when we were dropping our bombs over Dortmund or Cologne? I was far too preoccupied with calculating a wind for the bomb-aimer and a course for the pilot to think of much else – apart from my access to safety hatches and the security of my parachute harness in case I had to bale out. It is true that nearly two-thirds of the missions I flew were small-scale, highly focused affairs to bomb oil and ball-bearing production plants. This was not of my choosing though, and however precise our bombing, there was invariably some 'collateral' damage.

This chapter is not an essay in self-justification but a reflection on one of the defining experiences of my life. Moral concern about Bomber Command's offensive has grown rather than diminished over the years, a troublesome undercurrent to our national life that erupts once a year when Dresden is remembered on 13 February. Some reflection now, by someone who was actually there, may not be altogether out of place.

The entire nation was implicated in the bombers' war. What is outrageous is that those who carried out the policy and faced the danger should be required to carry the guilt – always apologetic, rather shame-faced, perhaps keeping quiet, especially when Dresden comes up. After 1945 I had to get on with the rest of my life and I had no more contact with the RAF. However, I have often been made to feel a degree of personal guilt, especially when I was working in East Africa, often closely with (still quite young) Christian missionaries who had spent the war comfortably distant in the Kenya Highlands.

I have tried in this memoir, as honestly as I can, to uncover the various levels of meaning that the war had for me as I moved towards active involvement, survived, and moved on. But it is a close-up, an internal view, as 'seen from the astrodome'. There are other perspectives and perhaps deeper levels of meaning that are available to me now. It is time for me to face the moral issue head-on.

The bombers' war was always morally problematic and Churchill, who had been its strongest supporter, was trying to distance himself from it at the end. There is no doubt that one of its central aims was to break the will of the German people; if serious damage could also be done to industrial production, well and good. For a long time, however, Bomber Command lacked the navigational expertise to locate and bomb relatively small industrial sites. When it was able to engage in much more focused precision bombing it did so, but 'area bombing', aimed at civilian morale, continued to the end.

Whatever the moral questions, in 1939 and 1940 this method of waging war seemed to make excellent sense. When the Germans bombed Warsaw in September 1939 Poland appeared to surrender overnight: this was a victory that was extremely economical in terms of human life. When Germany bombed Rotterdam in May 1940, Holland immediately capitulated; and the mere threat of bombing Paris appeared to achieve the surrender of France. Bombing, it seemed to the onlooking world, actually worked. If cities of high symbolic importance were the target, victory and peace could be attained with a minimum loss of life. The message seemed clear: bombing was not a recipe for mass slaughter but precisely the way to avoid it. Unfortunately, we had not reckoned on the astounding courage and resilience of the German people under massive and sustained attack, which makes the bombing of Warsaw and Rotterdam seem utterly trivial.

Where do we locate the bombing offensive along the moral continuum of methods of war? For clearly, and I would maintain self-evidently, some methods are relatively 'pure' (unless we are pacifists), while at the other extreme some fall right off the scale (see page 101). At the 'pure' end at the top of the moral scale we have evenly matched, face-to-face, hand-to-hand fighting with a sword or a lance (and without covering fire tank against tank); at the opposite pole we have unmanned (non-nuclear) intercontinental missiles (for instance a 'scud'); and off the scale altogether are hydrogen bombs and other (chemical and biological) 'weapons of mass destruction'. Between the poles which mark the ends of the scale are various positions and degrees of morality. I would place the Second World War bomber offensive in Europe carried out by the RAF and the American Eighth Air Force about halfway along – roughly in the same position as a siege or blockade.

Much has been said over the centuries about 'the just war' (*ius ad bellum*) – the moral and legitimate reasons for going to war; relatively little has been said about the morality and propriety of the various forms of fighting once war has begun (*ius in bellum*). In the Hague Conventions of 1899 and 1907, the Great Powers agreed to laws of war that prohibited the use of poison gas (although Germany used it in April 1915 and the British quickly followed suit). More informally, a French engineer, Sébastien le Prestre, Seigneur de Vaubon, outlined in his late seventeenth century *Traité sur l'Attaque des Places* rules for conducting a siege, which were widely adopted in the eighteenth century, notably in Marlborough's campaigns. A long tradition of chivalry that predated but was reinforced by the Crusades was nurtured by the troubadours who celebrated the virtues of the Christian knight: a code of conduct often honoured in the breach, but of considerable influence on medieval military courts. (The Norman minstrel Taillefer sang the *Chanson de Roland* on the field of battle at Hastings in 1066.)

The chivalric code defined the role of honour and valour in military encounters, the importance of equality in numbers (and armaments) of combatants, promoted gallantry towards women, and set out rules for ransoming prisoners. The fate of prisoners without wealth or rank, it is true, was rather more ambiguous. However, the management of ransom money – often of huge proportions – was highly regulated and largely in the hands of the great international finance houses. War in the age of chivalry (including the Crusades) was about plunder and a good return on investment as much as about honour. The generally accepted rules of dividing up the spoils of war and the share to be received by commanders (once set at a half, later reduced to a third) were the principal concern of Europe's military courts. Nevertheless, it is the echo down the centuries of the chivalric code that today shapes our perception of Bomber Command.

For all war's rapacity, systematic devastation and organisation as a highly successful protection racket, commanders in the age of chivalry would have found the concept of 'unconditional surrender' utterly abhorrent, indeed unintelligible. A peace settlement might even be agreed on the outcome of a carefully staged single combat – at least the proposal was often seriously made. For all the pillage of wealthy towns and great estates and the rape of women, the men would have found equally abhorrent the 'area bombing' of civilians, mainly women and children. It is true that King Edward I espoused Arthurian values but nevertheless imprisoned the Countess of Buchan and Robert Bruce's sister, Mary, in public cages on the castle walls of Berwick and Roxburgh. However, in 1346, after the English had captured Caen, Thomas Holland, Earl of Kent, with a few of his knights, rode on to the streets and collected up the young women to save them from rape by England's victorious archers. Six hundred years later, on the evening of 7 July 1944, 450 Lancasters and Halifaxes bombed Caen. Montgomery had failed to take the town from the Germans and Eisenhower had suggested 'area bombing' as an answer to deadlock. The war in fact was very little advanced by this act (Montgomery still failed to establish a bridgehead over the Orne). The main consequence of 2000 tons of high explosives was that the heart of the town was reduced to a mountain of rubble and an uncounted number of 'collateral casualties' occurred among the town's women and children. The British Army, looking on from their slit trenches, cheered.

The early medieval papacy proscribed the use of missiles by Christian knights, although its edicts were blatantly flouted by England's King Richard the Lionheart in the Third Crusade. In his ardent use of the powerful artillery piece, the crossbow, Richard fell significantly below the highest standards of his class:

only the lance and the sword (a crucifix) had a rightful place on the field of chivalry. In practice, slings, bows and arrows, and siege engines which could project highly destructive missiles, were in common use on the crusades, although only close-quarters' hand-to-hand fighting was thought appropriate for knights. The tournament and the duel are stylised 'civilian' models, which have enshrined and perpetuated the gentlemanly ideal.

The medieval papacy knew that distance blunts moral awareness; it will inevitably prevent a man from seeing the consequences of his actions. He will not witness the pain and disfigurement, devastation and death that he has caused. The most bellicose of national leaders have seldom seen the face of battle. The Emperor Napoleon III of France, unblooded in war, was all in favour of military solutions and glory; but a hasty truce with Austria at Villafranca quickly followed his personal experience of battle at Solferino. To the consternation of his Italian ally, Cavour, overnight he had become an ardent convert to peace.

There is a sharp moral contrast between the purity of hand-to-hand combat with swords, rapiers and lances (or even pistols) and the use of projectiles and missiles. With the use of slings, crossbows, cannon, muskets, rifles and finally rockets, the distance between combatants grows: they may not even be in the same continent. Distance is roughly proportional to morality. Stratospheric bombing from heights that make you totally invisible and virtually invulnerable is in a different and morally inferior league to bombing at lower levels through flak and fighter defences at 20,000 feet. The tainted image of the sniper is a simple, more humdrum example of this moral decline.

Distance between opposing sides on the one hand, and civilians as targets on the other, are two key issues in the morality of the conduct of war. There is a third – reasonable equality between the two sides, so that one does not simply slaughter the other. The issue of balance or equality was another of the cardinal principles of chivalry – again often honoured in the breach, but sometimes implemented with great formality and care: the two sides deliberately and systematically equalised before battle began. Single combat was sometimes proposed and even fought to settle a war between two nations; larger but equal units were also used. In 1341 a battle was arranged between the French and Bretons with two hundred selected soldiers on each side. In 1351 there was the famous 'fight of the thirty', an elaborately staged battle with a half-time interval for drinks. However, really important issues were probably never settled by such 'artificial' means.

The ideal of balanced forces is nevertheless a powerful one not only of chivalry but of natural justice. It is really about being, or not being, a bully. We shall judge a battle higher in the moral scale if it is won against a well matched, adequate defence. This principle is dramatised in the David and Goliath story. It provides a third criterion for calibrating the moral spectrum of war.

Warfare had changed dramatically in character over the centuries and not only because of technological advances. Today's armies are first and foremost killing machines. Earlier armies – before, say, the eighteenth century – had additional purposes to slaughter (although in wars of religion slaughter was always a very high priority). The battles were commercial enterprises, a means of securing booty, land, lucrative prisoners, and opening up new markets. The armies often fought to harass rather than to kill; and fighting to the death was not a requirement of duty or honour. Even Sir Francis Drake broke off from sinking the Spanish Armada ships to pursue richly laden prize ships when they presented themselves in the Channel sailing to Dutch ports. (There is, perhaps, an echo of this more pragmatic concept of war in the way British Army officers in the Crimea resigned their commissions when the going got rough and went home.) Armies as single-purpose killing machines came with the regiments of the eighteenth century: well drilled, highly disciplined, with a strong sense of loyalty and duty to their colonel and king. It is the uncompromising single-mindedness of modern armies that makes ancient criteria of chivalrous conduct not, in fact, superfluous but of heightened relevance and significance.

The 'pure' end of the moral spectrum of war is in practice an unattainable ideal: face-to-face combat; near equality (in numbers and armament) of opposing forces; and the total exclusion of civilians, especially women and children. At the

THE MORAL SCALE* : IUS IN BELLUM

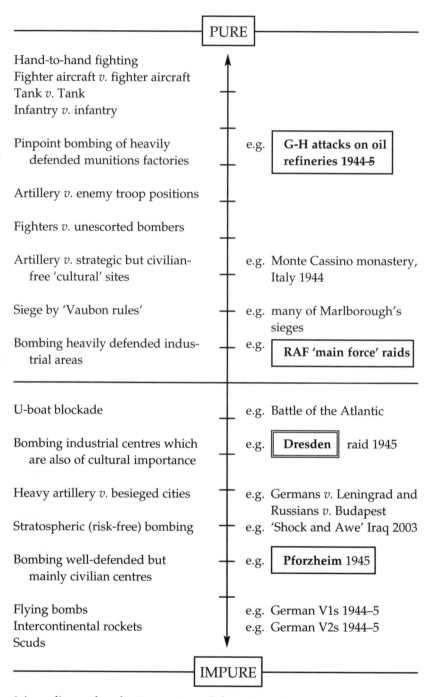

PURE

Hand-to-hand fighting
Fighter aircraft *v.* fighter aircraft
Tank *v.* Tank
Infantry *v.* infantry

Pinpoint bombing of heavily
    defended munitions factories

e.g. **G-H attacks on oil
refineries 1944-5**

Artillery *v.* enemy troop positions

Fighters *v.* unescorted bombers

Artillery *v.* strategic but civilian-
    free 'cultural' sites

e.g. Monte Cassino monastery,
Italy 1944

Siege by 'Vaubon rules'

e.g. many of Marlborough's
sieges

Bombing heavily defended indus-
    trial areas

e.g. **RAF 'main force' raids**

U-boat blockade

e.g. Battle of the Atlantic

Bombing industrial centres which
    are also of cultural importance

e.g. **Dresden** raid 1945

Heavy artillery *v.* besieged cities

e.g. Germans *v.* Leningrad and
Russians *v.* Budapest

Stratospheric (risk-free) bombing

e.g. 'Shock and Awe' Iraq 2003

Bombing well-defended but
    mainly civilian centres

e.g. **Pforzheim** 1945

Flying bombs
Intercontinental rockets
Scuds

e.g. German V1s 1944–5
e.g. German V2s 1944–5

IMPURE

* According to three basic criteria:- 1. Balance/imbalance of forces;
2. Distance between opponents; 3. Civilian involvement: nature and extent

other extreme there is a situation that could be only too easily realised: intercontinental missiles randomly targeting civilian populations in weak countries that are no match for the aggressor. Entirely off the scale, by universal consensus, are atomic weapons (though of course they were on the scale in August 1945). However, they are held, somewhat illogically, to be highly effective in deterrence (even though they can never actually be used). They are so massively destructive of human life and damaging to the environment that they cannot be located on any scale of morality in the means of waging war. They are simply off limits.

A position at the pole of purity could be artificially contrived; in practice, even the flower of English chivalry at Crécy, Poitiers and Agincourt fought dismounted with the covering support of archers. Mounted warfare between equal numbers of men with lances was no way to achieve victory. Fairly near to the pole of purity we can locate the Battle of Britain in 1940, El Alamein in 1942 and the Battle of Kursk in 1943: single-seater fighter against single-seater fighter, tank against tank. The tank and the single-seater fighter are the modern equivalent of a horse.

Of course, it was far more complicated than that. All three battles contained 'foreign' or 'impure' elements and fell somewhat short of the ideal. All involved a large measure of head-on (if not hand-to-hand) fighting at close quarters between well matched opponents in battles that almost entirely excluded civilians as targets or even as 'collateral' casualties. It is true that at El Alamein Montgomery's army was almost twice as large as Rommel's (which in any event was composed largely of Italians); and that the Battle of Kursk was not only T-34 tanks pitted against Tiger tanks, but involved significant use of Russian dive-bombers with tank-busting cannon and anti-tank bombs; and that in the Battle of Britain the German bombers that were attacked over England by Hurricanes and Spitfires were, for all their fighter cover, sitting ducks. Nevertheless, the three battles – even Kursk in its unspeakable ferocity and no quarter given – measure up quite well to the highest requirements of purity and *ius in bellum*. Purity can easily coexist with ferocity. It cannot coexist with such a grotesque imbalance of forces that you can slaughter at will and have no body bags of your own.

The Battle of Britain was fought between equal numbers of single-seater fighters of comparable technical performance: about 800 on each side at the beginning and, with continuous replacements, roughly the same number of aircraft (and pilots) on each side at the end. The skies over southern England were full of enemy aircraft: they were mainly quite slow and ungainly bombers, which the less sophisticated Hurricanes (rather then the Spitfires) were directed to attack. This was no contest (and in fact the 'inferior' Hurricanes had fewer losses than the 'superior' Spitfires). In the contest between fighters the battle was much more even, and so was the outcome. As the historian Richard Overy has concluded, for the RAF it was only 'a victory of sorts'. It was probably not the reason Germany did not invade Britain. Its main result was simply to divert German bombing from daytime to night. Fighter Command and its pilots will – in spite of relatively light losses – always occupy the moral high ground.

There are three methods of war that deliberately target civilians, attempt to undermine their well-being and destroy their morale: the siege, the blockade and area bombing. They are all fought at a distance: the soldiers, sailors and airmen do not see at close quarters, and perhaps not at all, the suffering they have caused. These engagements may or may not be 'in balance': the defences may be equal to or stronger than the attack. In that case the engagement can be located somewhat higher up the moral scale of war. However, the siege, the blockade and bombing will never approach the top of the scale.

The siege is a very ancient and common means of conducting war, sometimes directed against mainly military personnel in fortresses and castles, but more often against the civilian population of cities. City walls have offered provocation as much as protection, an invitation to military architects to devise ingenious means of breaching them. The siege has arisen with civilisation and urbanisation: it was hardly feasible in societies of nomadic horsemen without permanent encampments. Opulent centres of settled populations have been the usual victims of siege warfare: from Agamemnon's ten-year siege of the great Mycenaean city Troy, more than a thousand years before the birth of Christ, down to the German siege of Leningrad from 1941 to 1944.

Siege warfare aims to cut off food and fuel and other necessities of life from a mainly civilian population: it usually involves bombardment, starvation and eventually virulent disease. The great and wealthy Phoenician city, Carthage, on the Gulf of Tunis, with a population of around 700,000, was besieged by the Romans for three years in the Third Punic War. It was a determined and protracted assault on a concentrated civilian population, which ended only when the city was destroyed. The Crusades saw marked advances in the technology of siege warfare. In the Crusader states highly paid military engineers had an honoured place and developed siege towers and formidable 'mongonels' for projecting large stones. In the First Crusade Jerusalem was famously besieged, in the Third Acre, and infamously in the Fourth, the rich (Greek) Christian city, Constantinople.

The siege assumed a legendary importance in the Boer War with the relief of Ladysmith and Mafeking. The 110-day Prussian siege of Paris in 1870 demonstrated the horrors and potency of siege warfare at the very heart and centre of the civilised western world. The horrific culmination of siege warfare came with the German's 900-day siege of Leningrad from late 1941 to early 1944. A million noncombatants died. The German high command ordered the complete obliteration of the city and destruction of its population by bombing, shelling, starvation and disease. No surrender was to be accepted. The aim was annihilation. From a population of two-and-a-half million around 850,000 were evacuated; in the space of two-and-a-half years more than 50 per cent of those who remained were killed. This was a massacre of civilians on a scale without precedent in human history, conducted in one of the world's great centres of civilisation. Until the tide of war began to turn along the entire eastern front, German superiority in conducting the siege was wholly disproportionate. Its superiority over the inadequately defended city was deployed relentlessly and without mercy. This was siege warfare at a very low point on the scale of *ius in bellum*.

Like the siege, the blockade is primarily an attack on civilians, but much more 'at a distance'. During the Second World War it was conducted with complete invisibility from the depths of the sea. The German U-boat blockade of Britain was the most serious threat that we faced; and Churchill was fully aware of its gravity when, on 6 March 1941, he announced that we were now fighting 'the battle of the Atlantic'. In that battle U-boats killed 32,000 (civilian) British merchant navy seamen and in 1941–2 all but throttled the British people. (In 1938 our imports of food, fuel and other vital supplies totalled 68 million tons; in 1941 Britain lost 1300 ships and imported only 26 million tons.) By 1943, however, our defence by sea and air was containing the U-boat onslaught on our morale and well-being: for a short period of time we were sinking more than twenty U-boats a month. Over the course of the war 784 German submarines were lost and 27,490 submariners were killed (almost exactly half of the number killed in Bomber Command).

How do we evaluate these statistics? Like all the statistics of war they are virtually meaningless unless we see them in comparative terms. The U-boat losses were certainly seen by Admiral Dönitz and his submarine crews as formidable. How do they compare with those of Bomber Control?

In May 1943 forty-one German U-boats were sunk, each with a crew of between forty and fifty: around 1700 men were killed. This was unprecedented and Admiral Dönitz considered the losses unacceptable and unsustainable. He called a temporary halt to the U-boat campaign and withdrew his submarines from the Atlantic. In the same month Bomber Command lost 253 four-engined bombers, each with a crew of seven – a loss of 1770 men. This was an average month and nothing remarkable, certainly no reason for Harris to halt the campaign. Indeed, over the next fourteen months losses never fell below 1500 men and were often over 2000. The 1770 bomber-crew losses in May were from a total force of around 7000 aircrew; the 1700 submariner losses were from a total force of about 15,000. Dönitz had built up his fleet to over 300 vessels (about ninety of them would at any one time be patrolling the Atlantic). However we look at it, Bomber Command casualties were on a significantly greater scale than those of the German U-boats, even in their period of greatest peril.

Nevertheless, the German U-boat offensive was well balanced (eventually) by the defending forces of the opposing side; the men paid a high price for their onslaught, and stand proud in the annals of courage in war. Like Bomber Command the U-boats were engaged in 'blind killing' at a distance. Submariners could envisage themselves as being in the business of sinking ships rather than killing people. The Allied bombing of Europe and the German submarine attack on the entire British people have many relevant similarities and stand close together on any scale of the morality of war.

The Allied bombing of Germany was responsible for the deaths of some 600,000 civilians: approaching 1 per cent of the entire German nation. But this was only half as many civilians as the Germans killed in their two-and-a-half year siege of Leningrad. The deaths of Russian civilians in Leningrad totalled some 50 per cent of the city's population.

Like the German U-boat campaign, the bomber offensive was directed very largely against civilians; it was waged from a distance, against people the crews could not see. However, it was fought at a cost that by all contemporary and historical standards was very high and called for great endurance and courage. The bombing offensive and the U-boat campaign cannot stand anywhere near the top of my moral scale; but they are not at the bottom either. I would put them together about halfway along.

The American bombing campaign against Japan in the first half of 1945, before the atomic bombs were dropped, must be located much further down the moral scale, not far from the bottom – just a little higher than unmanned (non-nuclear) intercontinental missiles. America had now occupied Pacific islands from which heavy bombers could fly easily and with impunity to Japan. From April to August 1945, B-29 Super fortresses under the command of General Curtis LeMay attacked sixty-six Japanese cities and destroyed 40 per cent of their built-up areas through firestorms caused by incendiary bombs. The terrified city populations fled to the hills. The aircraft could bomb with negligible losses from 7000 feet. By August the Japanese high command was discussing surrender: the war in fact was over. There was no need for an atomic bomb to be dropped on Hiroshima (which President Harry Truman actually described as a 'military base'). There was certainly no need for the bombing of Nagasaki. But atomic bombing aside, General LeMay's conventional area bombing must rank very low on the scale of morality in the conduct of war, in a way that RAF Bomber Command and the American Eighth Air Force's actions in Europe do not.

I have tried, sixty years on, to see the bombers' war over Europe (and my own very modest part in it) in some kind of comparative, moral prospective. I believe that our reasons for mounting the bombers' war in the first place were powerful and good (*ius ad bellum*), but the actual tactics are far more question- able (*ius in bellum*). Although there was little choice other than 'area bombing' in the early stages, improved navigational methods offered more options later on, which could have been more fully exploited. The bomber's war does not come anywhere near the top of my moral scale; but it is certainly not at the bottom. As far as the aircrew are concerned, it was fought with astonishing gallantry.

I have tried to be dispassionate; I have also tried to devise some simple tools for handling the debate. My argument and my method of developing it are no doubt seriously flawed. For me, the simple test will always be the Witten sortie in December 1944: eight from a small force of Lancasters were destroyed by a handful of enemy fighters; fifty-six young men dead in a battle four miles high lasting about ten minutes. We had flown know- ingly into a situation where we were completely outgunned: a .303-in machine-gun pitted against a 20 mm cannon is simply no contest. Not a single German fighter was shot down. The final score was fifty-six to nil. In my book that will for ever vindicate Bomber Command.

To sum up: it is not the morality of Bomber Command and the tactics it used that seriously concern me now; it is the misuse of the Command to pursue wider strategic and political ends. The Command's contribution to Russia's advance into Germany was probably not very great; but the real irony is that the signal success of Bomber Command in the summer of 1943 probably made possible a just, honourable and properly balanced peace. Instead, the Allies insisted on the barbaric notion of uncondi- tional surrender and extended the slaughter and destruction of war for nearly two years.

Why unconditional surrender? On the assumption, pre-
sumably, that the German government and perhaps the entire
German people, were uniquely wicked and deserved a fate
worse than any customarily endured by a vanquished nation.
There were to be no negotiated peace terms for them.
Unconditional surrender was the objective agreed by Roosevelt
and Churchill when they met at Casablanca in January 1943, and
bombing was given priority as a means of achieving it. This
remarkable, indeed infamous, decision was endorsed by the
British war cabinet and accepted by Stalin. When Bomber
Command won a resounding victory over Hamburg in July and
August the possibility of a peace settlement which it surely
opened up, was not even explored. The thunderous victory over
Hamburg would certainly not have led to Germany's unconditional surrender, but it could have paved the way to a sensible,
negotiated redistribution of power in Europe. Germany was
now seriously weakened (not only by the raid on Hamburg).
England was strong, and neither America nor even Russia was
in unequivocal ascendancy.

The great raids which constitute the 'Battle of Hamburg' were
a body blow to the German nation. This was Germany's second
city, not too far from Britain or too obscurely located to make it
an especially difficult target for Bomber Command. The impact
of 800 heavy bombers a night was awesome: probably about 75
per cent of the city was destroyed; firestorms raged; smoke rose
to 20,000 feet; convection currents produced winds of 100 mph
through the streets; the emergency services were totally over-
whelmed; and probably 55,000 people were killed. Bomber
Command losses were surprisingly light: in terms of aircraft lost
to sorties flown, the ratio was only about 2.8 per cent – rather
below the average of 3.0 for Bomber Command raids. Whatever
we may think of its morality – and the attacks were strictly in
line with Churchill and Roosevelt's Casablanca directive – this
was one of the great victories, whether on land, sea or in the air,
of the Second World War, and Germany was shaken. It was
followed by serious unrest, indeed panic, throughout the population of northern Germany, and Albert Speer, Hitler's
Armaments Minister, thought that such punishment must lead
Germany to sue for peace. 'It put the fear of God in me,' he

confessed in his memoirs. The *Luftwaffe* Chief-of-Staff, Hans Jeschonnek, considered that, compared with Hamburg, Russia's victory at Stalingrad was 'trifling'. Shortly afterwards he shot himself.

The pressure on Germany was now immense. In May we had achieved a decisive victory over the German U-boat campaign, which for three years had been the biggest single threat to England's survival. In July, while our bombers attacked Hamburg, the Battle of Kursk was being fought on the eastern front and Russia's slaughter of the German Army was on a titanic scale. This threefold success in the summer of 1943 should have been the prelude to peace. It is true that the Americans suffered a spectacular defeat in the air over Schweinfurt in August (and would do so again in October); but if ever there was a time to reach a just and balanced negotiated peace settlement with Germany it was now. The absurdity of 'unconditional surrender' precluded that, and when Stalin met Churchill and Roosevelt in Teheran in November, the moment had passed. After the battles of Stalingrad and Kursk, Stalin concluded that Russia could now, if necessary, and even preferably, achieve Germany's unconditional surrender all by itself. Death and destruction, the rape of Germany, would continue for another eighteen months and two alien superpowers would bestride Europe and indeed the world.

At 12 o'clock on 20 June 1945 I took off in an old Wellington bomber from an airfield in Northamptonshire for the industrial heartlands of Germany. This was not a bombing mission but a sightseeing tour. The war in Europe had now been over for five weeks and I was navigating an aircraft that carried half a dozen ground staff personnel. They were to see for themselves something of the results to which they in their fashion had contributed. These sightseeing flights were being organised from airfields across eastern England. We flew at low level over Essen and Cologne and other industrial cities beyond; we observed the blackened ruins, the rubble and the complete desolation extending mile after mile. We could see little sign of life, no movement in this vast, shattered landscape. We were looking at destruction on a scale without historical precedent.

We returned to the green heartlands of England, flying low

over trim market towns. They were tranquil and undisturbed, though perhaps a trifle shabby now, after six years without paint. We knew, of course, that there were blackened gaps and craters in the streets of a dozen English cities caused by the *Luftwaffe*'s bombs – I had seen them in London, Bristol, Southampton and Hull. But what we had just witnessed was of a different order of magnitude. The *Luftwaffe*'s raids had killed 61,000 people in the whole of the United Kingdom; in Germany, deaths that could be attributed to the RAF amounted to more than 600,000. In Coventry the symbol of the *Luftwaffe*'s infamy, 554 civilians were killed; in Hamburg our bombers killed around 55,000. The destruction of Germany to bring her to the point of unconditional surrender – quite apart from the savagery of the Russian advance to Berlin – seemed altogether dispropor-tionate. As we climbed down from our Wellington bomber we did not feel triumphant or elated. We were quiet, thoughtful and subdued.

What we had seen on our sightseeing tour was entirely out of scale, at odds with the broad symmetry that must underlie a just war, unless it is to be not a 'war' but a massacre. The war had gone on too long; destruction had been heaped on destruction. On top of the raid on Dresden – within ten days – had come the action on Pforzheim, when 300 heavy bombers attacked this unoffending town at 8000 feet and killed 17,000 citizens, nearly a fifth of its population. Another hundred young men of Bomber Command also died. Bomber Command's triumph came in the late summer of 1943. It should have been Europe's triumph too. Instead, a notion alien to the core values of Western chivalry prevailed – 'unconditional surrender' – an idea which Roosevelt said had suddenly occurred to him before he announced it, without consultation, at the Casablanca press conference. It spelt not only Germany's but Europe's defeat.

CHAPTER TWELVE

Postscript:
Dresden Again

After I had finished writing this memoir another book on the Dresden raid was published: Frederick Taylor's *Dresden: Tuesday 13 February 1945* (2004). I read it with eager expectation. It was reputed to be 'revisionist'. Two principal conclusions seemed to me to emerge from this dense, heavily researched book: that the number of people killed on 13 February 1945 was a good deal smaller than is commonly supposed, somewhere between 25,000 and 40,000; and that Dresden's armaments factories and importance as a communications centre made it 'by the standards of the time a legitimate target'. (The largest employer in Dresden by far was Zeiss Ikon, 'And it was a long time since that distinguished company had produced anything as innocent as a snapshot camera'.) I found nothing in this book at all surprising but was pleased that the views I had expressed in my memoir were broadly confirmed. I felt nevertheless that some final, updated reflections prompted by reading this book might not be out of place.

Taylor deals comprehensively with the raid and its aftermath, including the widespread moral unease. I am less surprised than he seems to be that the moral shock waves that radiated from Dresden were so readily absorbed and had a negligible impact on the course of the war. It was not until three weeks after the raid that Richard Stokes MP rose in the House of Commons on 6 March to express his disquiet. 'Is terror bombing now part of official government policy?' he asked. (He had actually been asking the same ironic question in various public utterances since 1942.) In fact, in the spring and summer of 1945 the world took the bombing of Dresden in its stride. Area bombing of Germany continued unabated; and six months after Dresden, Hiroshima and Nagasaki were destroyed by atom bombs.

This, I suggest, is worth some reflection. The Americans are a deeply moral people. It is true that their distance from active theatres of war protected them from direct exposure to the destructiveness of modern military action. Their homeland had also never (then) been bombed. But President Truman and his Secretary of State, Henry L. Stimson, had both fought on the Western Front (in the Field Artillery) in the First World War; and as the President flew from Brussels to Berlin on 15 July 1945 he had an apocalyptic overview of the desolation caused by bombing.

The new President of the United States of America was flying to a conference at Potsdam with Stalin and Churchill, and about to make a decision that he alone would take, without consulting his allies, on the deployment of the atomic bomb. The flight took three-and-a-half hours. Throughout, the President looked with fascination and rising horror on the desolation that unfolded below: shattered bridges, wrecked factories, entire cities in ruins. People were living like animals, he was told, scavenging for food. No President in American history had seen such a vista of devastation and despair. (He would see this at close quarters on the following day when the presidential motorcade toured the ruins of Berlin.) The President was carrying a shortlist of Japanese cities on which atomic bombs might be dropped, if bombing were, after all, to be decided. The list included Kyoto, a city of architectural distinction and historic cultural importance: the Japanese equivalent in fact (as Stimson was particularly aware) of Dresden.

The final tests at Alamogordo were successful. Atomic bombs were now ready for deployment. They would not win the war: it had to all intents and purposes already been won by conventional means. Henry L. Stimson was an elderly statesman of deep culture with a strong sense of the responsibilities of history. He had serious misgivings about bombs in general and atomic bombs in particular: 'modern civilisation might be completely destroyed.' He was an austere, old-fashioned man, deeply concerned about 'the moral advancement of the world'.

He conferred earnestly with the President who agonised over the decision for a week. A full awareness of Dresden and a panoramic view of bombed-out Germany carried insufficient weight: the final decision was to proceed with the bombing. There was, however, one gesture towards Dresden – Kyoto would be saved.

Frederick Taylor advances in his book a simple theory of technological determinism. He states it more elaborately, but put quite simply it is: 'If they've got it they'll use it' (and only massive deterrence is likely to prevent it). The series of events I have detailed above seems to support the theory. I think a more likely explanation is not technological but political determinism. The momentum that had built up since the Manhattan project was inaugurated in 1942 was virtually unstoppable, and for President Truman to decide other than he did unthinkable. It is doubtless the mark of leadership to think the unthinkable and stop the unstoppable, to cut across the well established current of events; but it would have required monumental courage in a new and largely untried President to do so. No political leader (especially perhaps in a democracy) could halt the process that had been so long in train, had absorbed vast material and intellectual resources, and had underpinned, in the final analysis, a confident war effort that could insist on unconditional surrender.

The 'Father of the Royal Air Force', Lord Trenchard, had an even simpler theory of technological inevitability, and Taylor gives an interesting account of the way he developed and propounded it in the interwar years. Trenchard had been much impressed and dismayed by the protracted stalemate on the Western Front in the First World War and believed that only by bombing civilians in the hinterland could deadlock be broken. In a future war between great and powerful industrial nations, deadlock would be inevitable and so therefore would bombing. In any future war the bombing of civilians would play a prominent, indeed decisive, part.

It is curious, therefore, that it was not deadlock but precisely the opposite that made the case for bombing Germany in 1939 and 1940. We were not deadlocked with an enemy of roughly equal weight in an indecisive pounding match: we were in full flight from an enemy of obvious superiority. Taylor seems to be unaware of this oddity in his apparently approving, or at least neutral, commentary on Trenchard's theories.

Rather than advancing sophisticated military theories, Trenchard was softening up the moral outlook not only of the warrior class but the entire nation. 'The nation that would stand being bombed the longest would win in the end,' he announced, as if bombing entire nations was rather a matter of course. Trenchard was engaging in a form of discourse which made the systematic and sustained bombing of civilian populations seem not only inevitable but normal. He was remarkably frank: 'It is on the destruction of enemy industries and, above all, the lowering of morale . . . by bombing that ultimate victory rests.'

Events have a way of appearing inevitable once they have occurred, and even the outcome of some underlying law of historical determinism. However, at the time they happen there are choices, sometimes very restricted, at others more numerous. Britain's choices in 1939 and especially in 1940 were clearly very restricted indeed: not to use bombers however and whenever we could was simply not an option if we were to stay in the war. But the choices had widened enormously by 1943: even the choice to end the war justly and sensibly, although largely unrecognised, was now available. Certainly by 1944, area bombing should have been totally abandoned, Bomber Command drastically reduced in size and most of the aircrew and ground staff remustered or demobbed. A small bomber force would now engage in highly selective, pinpoint bombing of synthetic oil factories, steelworks, rocket-production plants and launch sites. Of course, events develop a powerful momentum and become encrusted with vested interests; but it was now necessary to cut across the current of events and reverse it. What we actually experienced from mid-1943 was a massive failure in leadership: a palpable lack of imagination, of intellect and political will.

Why? The principal reason for this was not the hidden hand of historical determinism that propelled events along their inexorable course, but the constraints of allies. The interplay between Britain, Russia and America, often choreographed on an international stage, kept the 'Allies' locked into courses of competitive awfulness. What we needed above all was not some corrosive 'openness' but old-fashioned secret diplomacy, not least with our enemy Germany. Instead, we had world theatre: at Casablanca, Teheran, Yalta and Potsdam. This was utterly disastrous: leadership was emasculated in the largely futile search for consensus.

At these conferences the great decisions were made and confirmed, although not necessarily jointly or after due consultation. At Casablanca the requirement of unconditional surrender was announced, and bombing as our principal instrument of war confirmed; Teheran reinforced 'second frontism' and the continuation of war until this was achieved; at Yalta the eastern programme of bombing, which included Dresden, was endorsed; at Potsdam Truman decided to drop atom bombs on Japan. Even when unilateral decisions were made, whether at press conferences or in secret, the competitive, hostile ambience of these conferences kept awfulness alive and on track. Potsdam was the start of the Cold War. This international posturing was a calamity: the war should in any case have been over before the second conference was convened. As it was, the full set of meetings lengthened the war and intensified its horrors. The conferences contrived and confirmed the dismemberment of Germany and the enslavement of eastern Europe. There is scarcely a redeeming feature that it is possible to cite.

There is undoubtedly always a strain towards making the most effective use of the technology that you've got. However, in practice civilised countries have usually punched less than their weight: they have fought with one arm tied behind their back. There are customs, traditions, ideals, sometimes more formal agreements that have constrained behaviour: self-imposed limitations that may well have delayed victory. States have accepted limits to what they may do in order to win. There is civilised war. Victors do not kill their enemies if they have laid down their arms and formally surrendered, however much of an encumbrance they might be; nor do they torture them. Once upon a time civilians, commonly the victims of war, were only incidental ('collateral') casualties. They were not prime targets who, on the Trenchard doctrine, would be selected for discomfiture and death as a principal method of winning.

Values intervene, and they, as well as technology and practicality influence action. In land warfare 'enemy' civilians are often an obstruction, simply cluttering up the action (although they may also be a source of support, shelter and supplies); at one extreme they may be gathered up into safe havens away from the areas of battle, at the other extreme they may be exterminated. There are various positions between these extremes from interdependency to coexistence and parallelism (quite common in relatively static, highly formalised warfare) to deportation and enslavement. (Rape is normal, plunder and arson common – all three are usually proscribed, but even the most conscientious and effective commander has difficulty with preventing rape, as Wellington knew full well after finally taking Badajós.)

The Russians simply exterminated the civilian population of East Prussia in April and May 1945 as they advanced to Berlin: a population of 2.2 million was reduced to 200,000 – literally deci-mated. (The bombing campaign eliminated 1 per cent of the German population; the Russians in East Prussia eliminated 90 per cent.) Safe havens were Kitchener's solution in the Boer War: they were called concentration camps. They were at first seriously mismanaged and thousands died from disease; but the Boer leader, General Botha, conceded in April 1902 that he was 'only too thankful to know that our wives are under British protection'. When Kitchener reversed his policy and ceased to bring women and children into the camps the Boer war effort was seriously impeded and British victory at last assured. The opposition leaders in England – Campbell-Bannerman and George – had denounced the war conducted by the British Army as barbarism and even genocide. This was in fact the final flourish of a thousand years of the chivalric tradition. (Kitchener had two Australian officers executed for their responsibility in the shooting of twelve Boer prisoners-of-war: the political fall-out was of course immense.) The real moral descent was still to come in the new century that was dawning.

The historian's diligent research which tries to establish 'what really happened' is invaluable; but a subject like Dresden, which is nothing if not a moral minefield, calls for much more. Taylor signally fails to give us this. He is well aware that his story raises huge moral issues, but he does little even to define them and nothing to solve them. Even his very interesting account of

Dresden's political and cultural history raises obvious moral questions such as: Dresden was special, but how do we weigh the bombing of 'Florence on the Elbe' with the bombing of Essen and Dortmund? Taylor offers no comment.

He concedes that matters dealt with in his book 'can and should unleash passionate moral and legal arguments', but he pulls back sharply from passion and refuses to enter the debate. He claims that his research revealed the Dresden raid in 'a much more complex and ambivalent moral framework than has hitherto been generally recognised'. He offers no guidelines or pointers in tackling this problem: 'The final moral judgement . . . remains, as it must, the reader's.' The author has opted out.

There was one relatively minor, but highly personal, moral conundrum that was of especial interest to me – the account that a bomb-aimer gave of his thoughts and actions over Dresden during the raid. He was one of four or five veterans who were interviewed by Taylor in the course of writing his book. The bomb-aimer – now a man in his eighties – says that as he guided his pilot on the bombing run he was appalled by the obvious firestorm raging below. For a time he was unable to hear the directions of the Master Bomber and decided that he would direct his pilot away from the central target area towards open country beyond the suburbs. And it was in open country that he dropped his bombs.

This bomb-aimer was a man of great courage. He was un-expectedly called upon to fly an extended tour and did so, flying to very difficult and heavily defended 'far-eastern' German targets, which included Chemnitz. However, I do not find his account of his bombing run over Dresden credible. After all this time he himself may well believe it; but I am profoundly saddened that he should have to give this version. It is a gloss on events by a man carrying the burden of sixty years of guilt, for a situation that was certainly not of his making. There is no shame in putting his bombs dead centre in the marked target area. The shame is the nation's, that a very brave man should have to say that he didn't. I have been tempted over the years to take part in this sort of evasion myself. I hope that I have not too often succumbed.

Of course, Dresden needs to be seen in a broader, comparative perspective. Perhaps it was a low point in a long moral decline? This would be a very difficult trend to substantiate. However, a significant general twentieth-century decline is what Norman Davies appears to be arguing in his recent broad historical survey, *Europe: a History* (1996). He characterises the three decades after 1914 as 'Europe in Eclipse'. This was a time of militaristic regimes, totalitarian states and total war, which produced '. . . an unequalled sum of death, misery and degradation'. In fact, says Davies, it was 'the era when Europe took leave of its senses'. This is not the most sophisticated analysis or interpretation of the circumstances he graphically describes, but it puts Dresden and area bombing in a context.

There was undoubtedly a seismic shift in the values of the warrior class – indeed, of what had become, through the pervasive influence of regimental networks, a warrior society – in the early twentieth century. Chivalric ideals and traditions were eroded in an age of triumphant cost-conscious, counting-house capitalism. The ancient ideals of chivalry had been strengthened in the early nineteenth century, after a colder climate in the Age of Reason. They had of course been ridiculed by Cervantes in *Don Quixote* and by Samuel Butler in *Hudibras*. The regimental ethos itself, with its emphasis on discipline, conformity and blind loyalty, as distinct from chivalric adventurousness, individualism and even eccentricity, also did something to undermine it. But Sir Thomas Malory's *Le Morte d'Arthur*, first published (by Caxton) in 1485, was reprinted in 1819 (the year in which Sir Walter Scott published *Ivanhoe*). It was carried by T.E. Lawrence in his saddlebag during the Arab Revolt and Siegfried Sassoon asked to hold it on his deathbed. Tennyson wrote *The Idylls of the King* and the Pre-Raphaelites (notably the socialist William Morris) celebrated and reaffirmed the military values of Arthurian romance. Public School chapels, encrusted with memorial plaques, had become mausoleums sanctifying death in battle; and a quarter of Wykehamists were choosing the Army as a career. War was ennobling when fought within the rules of a closely run cricket match played to a finish in a failing light. The Charge of the Light Brigade inspired a warrior nation: it was an echo of the Battle of Roncesvalles when Roland fought against impossible odds.

Gallantry has a way of being wasteful. No military commander today will willingly engage the enemy unless he has built up overwhelming superiority in men and weaponry. This is not cowardice; it is accountancy. A modern democracy with a conscript army demands nothing less. The Allies won the war principally because by 1943 their factories (especially America's) were producing three times more aircraft and tanks than the Axis powers, and four times more heavy guns. Morale (self-righteousness fed by the ceaseless rhetoric of freedom and democracy) was important too; but massively disproportionate armaments were the real foundation of success. Chivalry withers in such an entirely laudable climate of calculation of profit and loss and efficiency ratios of resources to death. Only a few relatively small forces, preferably of volunteers, can indulge the luxury of constant engagement against the odds. Bomber Command was one of them. Operating at the cutting edge of science and technology but wasteful in its usage of young lives, it was a throwback to an earlier age.

I discussed at the beginning of this memoir the role that the demand for unconditional surrender played in overkill. But to unconditional surrender we must surely add democracy and conscription. The pressure on the politicians and military commanders since the early twentieth century has been to finish war off quickly and get the boys back home. This kind of urgency has perhaps been stronger in America than Britain.

In the professional armies of the eighteenth and much of the nineteenth century, the 'boys' had no urgent desire to return home. Their home was indeed the regiment; a return to the family home usually meant a return to the scrap heap. War was a leisurely affair interrupted occasionally by diplomacy. Battles, even great victories, were seldom decisive: after the undoubted victory of Blenheim in 1704 a peace treaty was ten years away. (A peace treaty was also ten years down the line from Trafalgar.) Battles were fought in the summer season and in September armies retired to their winter quarters. (By the eighteenth century they no longer 'lived off the land' – their mobile bread ovens were enormous.) War was a way of life sometimes rudely interrupted by peace.

Since the Crimean War we have had greater 'openness' and

accountability in the conduct of war. Newspaper war reporters have arrived at the scene of combat and exposed the inefficiencies of a more casual way of war. In the Boer War well-meaning (and well-heeled) women 'screamers' – famously Emily Hobhouse and Millicent Fawcett – travelled to South Africa from comfortable middle-class homes and reported back to the people and their friends in Parliament. The pressure was on. What was needed was not gallantry but efficiency – not so much individual initiative as accountability. War was expensive: it mustn't last too long.

This is a look backwards, in order to see Dresden in a historical trend of shifting constraints and values; but we need to look forward, too, to the years beyond 1945. The supreme irony is that saturation bombing – the degradation and demoralisation of civilian populations to achieve political ends – has provided the basic model for constraining out-of-step states. Instead of killing their citizens with bombs, the United Nations routinely starves them to death. Sanctions are on par with Dresden. The policy of sanctions is saturation bombing by other means.

Iraq since 1990 is a topical case in point. During the Second World War bombing killed an estimated 600,000 German civilians in nearly six years; the UN killed an estimated one million Iraqis from a much smaller population (about twenty million) in eight years (1990–9) of sanctions.

This was the estimate made in 1998 by Dennis Halliday, the UN Humanitarian Coordinator for Iraq and former UN Assistant Secretary who resigned in protest. Sanctions dramatically reduced levels of nutrition and health care. In 1990 Iraq's per capita GNP was about $3000 but by 2001 it was less than $500. From being a very affluent society Iraq was now, in the space of a decade, one of the world's poorest countries. The 'oil-for-food' programme was too restrictive to make much difference to living standards; but most important of all the water supply system was seriously degraded. Restricted imports of water purification equipment and chemicals led to impure supplies and consequent disease and death.

Against perhaps 40,000 deaths in Dresden from bombing we must set a million deaths in Iraq caused by UN sanctions. The bombing of Germany killed roughly 1 per cent of the population, whereas sanctions imposed by the UN killed 5 per cent of Iraq's population (one million out of twenty million). This was about the same percentage of fatalities as was caused by Bomber Command in Dresden: about 40,000 deaths out of a population (including refugees) of about 800,000. In fact, with almost mathematical exactitude, Iraq equals Dresden.

The policy of sanctions, although less dramatic and on a different time scale, is in my opinion bombing by other means. It is not the way for an advanced civilisation to deal with 'rogue states' or recalcitrant regimes which refuse to bend to the will of the UN (or the United States). The first step is to find out why a rogue state is a rogue state, a regime recalcitrant, and a dictator a dictator. Dictatorship can be a perfectly reasonable solution to local problems, albeit deeply immoral in some Western eyes. (Of course, a dictatorship is always a conciliar government: it cannot all be done by one man, even with the help of his brothers and uncles.) When we have patiently explored and identified the underlying problems we may be able to find solutions short of starving everybody to death.

The scale of morality for military action that I tried to calibrate in my consideration of '*ius in bellum*' is a very basic tool. There are refinements that could and perhaps should be made. The first is the weighting of civilian involvement according to whether it is incidental ('collateral') or deliberately targeted; the second is the 'Monte Cassino' factor. Again, it is important to distinguish between deliberate destruction of architectural and other artistic works of great beauty and distinction (vandalism), and the incidental but inevitable damage arising from the 'legitimate' prosecution of war. Deliberate targeting of civilians and deliberate destruction of great architecture will push any military action much further down the moral scale. On Taylor's evidence Dresden can probably be cleared on both counts.

Nevertheless, the pressures of war were not such that Dresden must, at all costs, be attacked. The bombing of Dresden still comes significantly below the mid-point of my moral scale. To say, however, that it has fallen to the very bottom of my scale would be absurd. For that we must look more than three hundred miles to the south-east of Dresden. On the very same day, Tuesday 13 February, the Russians, with unspeakable ferocity, finally took and destroyed (after a siege lasting since Christmas) the historic city of Budapest. For good measure we might also look a hundred or so miles to the north where the Red Army advanced into East Prussia. To the south-east and the north of Dresden, what was in progress was genocide. The slaughter, enslavement and destruction was massive, deliberate, vindictive, brutal and primitive. In the ancient Hungarian capital on the Danube, which had been under relentless bombardment for fifty days, the events of Tuesday 13 February were singularly horrendous. In the words of the author Antony Beevor, 'The end of this terrible battle for the city was marked by an orgy of killing, looting, destruction and rape'. This is in a moral class all of its own. On 13 February the whole of Western Europe should remember these events in Budapest as well as reflect deeply on Dresden. We should all resolve to do whatever it takes to prevent such debasement and degradation of a thousand years of Western European civilisation ever happening again.

References

Chandler, David, *Marlborough as Military Commander* (Batsford 1984)

Corrigan, Gordon, *Mud, Blood and Poppycock* (Cassell 2003)

Froissart, Jean, *Chronicles* (Penguin Books 1968)

Hastings, Max, *Bomber Command* (Michael Joseph 1979)

Irving, David, *The Destruction of Dresden* (Kimber 1963)

Keegan, John, *A History of Warfare* (Hutchinson 1993)

Kemp, Paul, *U-Boats Destroyed: German Submarine Losses in the World Wars* (Arms and Armour 1997)

McKee, Alexander, *The Devil's Tinderbox: Dresden 1945* (Souvenir Press 1982)

Middlebrook, Martin, *The Nuremberg Raid* (Allen Lane 1973)

—*Arnhem 1944*   (Viking 1994)

—*The Berlin Raids*   (Cassell 2000)

—*The Bomber Command War Diaries*   (Penguin Books 1990)

Nicolle, David, *The Crusades* (Osprey 1988)

Overy, Richard, *Why the Allies Won* (Jonathan Cape 1995)

—*The Battle*   (Penguin Books 2000)

Palmer, Alan, *Victory 1918* (Weidenfeld & Nicolson 1998)

Prestwich, Michael, *The Three Edwards: War and State in England 1272–1377* (Methuen 1981)

Probert, Henry, *(Bomber Harris. His Life and Times* (Greenhill Books 2003)

Schumpeter, Joseph A., *Capitalism, Socialism and Democracy* (George Allen & Unwin 1976)

Sebald, W.G., *On the Natural History of Destruction* (Hamish Hamilton 2003)

Taylor, A.J.P., *The Course of German History* (Hamish Hamilton 1945)

Terraine, John, *The Right of the Line* (Hodder and Stoughton 1985)

ADDITIONAL REFERENCES

Barthorp, Michael, *The Anglo-Boer Wars* (Blandford Press 1987)

Beevor, Antony, *Berlin: The Downfall 1945* (Penguin Books 2003)

Davies, Norman, *Europe: a History* (OUP 1996)

McCullough, David, *Truman* (Simon & Schuuster NY, 1992)

Pakenham, Thomas, *The Boer War* (Abacus 1992)

Taylor, Frederick, *Dresden: Tuesday 13 February 1945* (Bloomsbury 2004).

Index